T0328600

Cambridge Elements

Elements in Ancient Egypt in Context
edited by
Gianluca Miniaci
University of Pisa
Juan Carlos Moreno García
CNRS, Paris
Anna Stevens
University of Cambridge and Monash University

EGYPTIAN ARCHAEOLOGY AND THE TWENTY-FIRST CENTURY MUSEUM

Alice Stevenson
UCL Institute of Archaeology

CAMBRIDGE
UNIVERSITY PRESS

CAMBRIDGE
UNIVERSITY PRESS

Shaftesbury Road, Cambridge CB2 8EA, United Kingdom

One Liberty Plaza, 20th Floor, New York, NY 10006, USA

477 Williamstown Road, Port Melbourne, VIC 3207, Australia

314–321, 3rd Floor, Plot 3, Splendor Forum, Jasola District Centre, New Delhi – 110025, India

103 Penang Road, #05–06/07, Visioncrest Commercial, Singapore 238467

Cambridge University Press is part of Cambridge University Press & Assessment, a department of the University of Cambridge.

We share the University's mission to contribute to society through the pursuit of education, learning and research at the highest international levels of excellence.

www.cambridge.org
Information on this title: www.cambridge.org/9781009074377

DOI: 10.1017/9781009070348

First published 2022

A catalogue record for this publication is available from the British Library.

ISBN 978-1-009-07437-7 Paperback
ISSN 2516-4813 (online)
ISSN 2516-4805 (print)

Egyptian Archaeology and the Twenty-First Century Museum

Elements in Ancient Egypt in Context

DOI: 10.1017/9781009070348
First published online: August 2022

Alice Stevenson
UCL Institute of Archaeology

Author for correspondence: Alice Stevenson, alice.stevenson@ucl.ac.uk

Abstract: This Element addresses the cultural production of ancient Egypt in the museum as a mixture of multiple pasts and presents that cohere around collections; their artefacts, documentation, storage, research, and display. Its four sections examine how ideas about the past are formed by museum assemblages: how their histories of acquisition and documentation shape interpretation, the range of materials that comprise them, the influence of their geographical framing, and the moments of remaking that might be possible. Throughout, the importance of critical approaches to interpretation is underscored, reasserting the museum as a site of active research and experiment, rather than only exhibitionary product or communicative media. It argues for a multi-directional approach to museum work that seeks to reveal the interrelations of collection histories and which has implications not just for museum representation and documentation, but also for archaeological practice more broadly.

Keywords: museums, exhibitions, museum decolonization, histories of collection, museum archaeology

ISBNs: 9781009074377 (PB), 9781009070348 (OC)
ISSNs: 2516-4813 (online), 2516-4805 (print)

Contents

1 Introduction

In 2010, a radio programme produced by the British Broadcasting Corporation (BBC) and the British Museum, *A History of the World in 100 Objects*, was aired, narrated by the then Director of the British Museum, Neil MacGregor. The initiative was enormously successful, garnering bestseller status for the accompanying book and providing a narrative model that was widely emulated. In the first episode, MacGregor outlined its rationale: 'In these programmes I'm travelling back in time and across the globe, to see how we humans, over two million years, have shaped our world, and been shaped by it'. (MacGregor 2010: xv).

Despite travelling far and wide, it is telling that the departure point for the entire series was an Egyptian coffin and the human remains it enclosed; 'the mummy of Hornedjitef' dating to around 240 BC (Figure 1). The choice implicitly recognized the cache that 'ancient Egypt' has as an iconic museum culture to be desired and consumed, and which has come to stand for the museum and for the idea of 'antiquity' itself (Meskell 2004: 179–207). The explicit justification for opening a view on the world with Hornedjitef's coffin was that it would help listeners and readers comprehend what it means to be human. But, as Riggs notes, to 'impose modern sensibilities onto ancient society implies that shared humanity equates to shared cultural values. It does not ... the complexity of how past and present intertwine is one of the legacies with which the object world endows us' (Riggs 2014: 221).

This Element takes up this challenge to examine such complexity by addressing the cultural production of ancient Egypt in the museum as a mixture of multiple pasts and presents that cohere around collections. In particular, it sets out to problematize the time and place of 'ancient Egypt' as an 'exotic chronotope' with both historical depth – a verticality that is both real and figurative – and a contemporary horizontality, a product of present contexts. How these layers are collapsed, teased apart, transcended, or otherwise placed into dialogue to inform constructs about Egypt through the museum is explored in four sections. These highlight the challenges of forming ideas about the past using museum assemblages: how their histories of acquisition and documentation shape interpretation; the range of materials that comprise them; the influence of where they are physically located and geographically framed, but also the moments of remaking that might be possible.

The role of museums in providing a sense of place, identity, and meaning for communities is a vital aspect of the contemporary museum sector, with new societal purposes being sought for such institutions in regard to well-being, activism, and social justice. Questions of ownership, repatriation, and

Figure 1 Coffin of Hornedjitef (museum number EA6678). Courtesy of the
Trustees of the British Museum

restitution are equally pressing topics. These are relevant and necessary
developments but although they are implicated in this Element, they are not
my primary focus. Rather, I seek throughout to demonstrate the importance of

critical approaches to interpretation, reasserting the significance of the museum as a site of active research, a place of interpretive process and experiment, rather than only exhibitionary product or communicative media. To these ends, I argue for a multi-directional approach to museum work that seeks to reveal the intertextuality of collection histories. With lateral thinking, this has implications not just for museum representation and documentation, but also Egyptological practice. Adopting a museum sensibility marshals for interdisciplinary projects the professional skills that have been developed in museum contexts. This includes navigating networks of related documentation, exploring juxtapositions of different media, and finding opportunities to intersect the multiplicity of voices that seek to understand the past. And because of museum commitments to public accountability and transparency, it also raises the very ethics of archaeological research. Therefore, questions that are raised across the museum sector and which have implications for how the Egyptian past is approached and constructed are also brought into discussion throughout.

1.1 The Twenty-First Century Museum

The European accumulation of Egyptian antiquities has a centuries' long history, but the vast majority of public Egyptology collections are today housed in museums established in the nineteenth or early twentieth centuries. Such institutions have been cast as sites of 'civilizing rituals', as a means of boosting the prestige of emergent nation states, and as arenas for the accumulation of cultural capital (Bennett 1995; Duncan 1995). As both a product and a tool of European colonial ideologies, the museum categorized, organized, and racialized the world, seeking to control and ultimately dominate world cultures within modernity's image. In so doing, they embedded social evolutionary conceptions of time and linear sequence at their core (see Section 2.1). This is a rather crude characterization of museum development given that no two museums are alike and that there are global differences in the social, cultural, and political contexts of institutional growth and decline. Indeed, the 'museum as monolith' has recently been challenged by studies that have examined the historical particularities behind the assembly of museum collections. These were not always reducible to imperial strategies or national status but involved a mix of personal agendas, local agencies, and historical happenstance (Křížová 2021; Morphy 2015). Nevertheless, as museums were increasingly professionalized, there was a widespread projection (not always realized) of an authority that was certain and a hierarchy of times and places that was deemed stable.

Attempts to characterize the twenty-first century museum, in contrast, are riven by a combination of anxiety and ambition. This was thrown into relief in 2019 when the International Council of Museums (ICOM) attempted, but failed, to agree upon a new definition of 'museum' (Mairesse 2019). Tensions emerged between those that wished to retain the importance of the supposed certainties of education, collecting, and conservation, and those that wanted an expanded, more aspirational, and critical remit, including social justice agendas and an attention to the politics of recognition. Such a 'crisis of authority' has deeper roots within the museum sector itself, often identified in the 1980s as a 'new museology' that took an interest not just in the methods of museums, but their purposes (Desvallées et al. 1992; Vergo 1989; but see Krstović 2020). Who museums were for, how they represented (or misrepresented) peoples and cultures, became foci for disciplinary introspection, as old convictions concerning fixed, bounded meanings dissolved. Disciplines such as archaeology and anthropology equally faced representational critique in these decades, as the inherently political and socially contingent nature of their practices was recognized. By the late 2010s, broader social movements such as Black Lives Matter, brought debates over museum authority into a more visible and immediate public global discourse (Szántó 2020). Significantly for this study, in being drawn into this 'global contemporary' (Knell 2019), foundational assumptions about time and history that have long organized the Eurocentric museum were destabilized (Clifford 2019).

One word in particular has coursed through disciplines, institutions, and museums worldwide; decolonization (Coombes and Phillips 2020). For some this translates into efforts towards more inclusive representation by, for, and about minoritized groups. But decolonization also requires addressing white Eurocentric voices that still make up the majority of both museum visitors and the discipline of Egyptology, by making transparent the histories that have profoundly shaped present circumstances and knowledge production, but which have been marginalized or neglected. Now there is still a vital project of decoloniality that needs to take place as part of decolonization – that is a radical exercise of 'un-thinking, de-disciplining, and re-educating' (Maldonado-Torres cited in Muñiz-Reed 2017) that establishes fresh research questions and frames of reference that do not necessarily derive from European thought or categories. It is not my intention to co-opt such scholarship, as there is another necessary first step as Minott advocates (2019); to challenge the notion of a museum as neutral space. It is this need to reveal the fundamental processes of the museum – the way it continues produce the data and frames of reference in use today – that is my focus in this Element.

Some Egyptologists are affronted by and explicitly reject the idea of decolonization (Gertzen 2021), where it has been seen as negative, simplistic, and confrontational. In what is reminiscent of challenges to disciplinary authority experienced by archaeology and anthropology in the late twentieth century, Egyptology's academic identity has been shaken. Decolonization cannot, however, simply be rejected. It is a contemporary discourse that cuts across disciplines in what is an intensified cultural moment of political action and redress based upon decades of campaigning by Indigenous peoples and civil-rights activists rather than just a theory or a metaphor (Tuck and Yang 2012). Decolonization is now fundamentally part of the lexicon of the twenty-first century museum sector, albeit one often appropriated or misunderstood as a form of additive diversification rather than as a central challenge to the structures underpinning institutional and disciplinary practice. It has equally been misconstrued as a reductive process. The prefix 'de', however, does not signal negation (which is impossible), rather it seeks to confront colonial histories with fresh perspectives.

The latter includes Egyptian perspectives. Contrary to erroneous assertions that 'any claim of modern Egyptians to "their" cultural heritage seems just as doubtful [as Coptic ancestry]' (Gertzen 2021: 194), there is a fundamental moral significance to foregrounding Egyptian viewpoints within decolonial agendas. What constitutes 'source communities' or 'communities of origin', is not simply reducible to kinship or ethnicity; they are equally fostered through long-term relationships to and lived experiences within landscapes and their histories, as indeed was emphasized by Egyptian political geographer Gamal Hamdan (1967). It refers to the groups in the past amongst which, and on whose labour, colonial administrators, archaeologists, and collectors operated, and it recognizes that these artefacts can play an important role in the identities of groups today (Peers and Brown 2003). The term is not without its issues, reasserting binary oppositions which dissolve when source community members also constitute professional or disciplinary communities. But as Peers (2014) has observed, the term has a directness that speaks to the global contemporary, the needs of redress, and the intractable tensions between groups.

In this regard, the history of Egyptian efforts to understand the ancient past has become an important subject of research (Colla 2007; Reid 2002; Riggs 2017b). Some redressive histories have focussed principally on Cairo-based institutions, such as the Antiquities Service, or elite Egyptians (who attempted or claimed to speak for Egyptian national interests). Other histories have brought attention to a broader range of individuals in Egyptian society, from *reises* to basket carriers, who had agency in the discovery, recovery, and excavation of artefacts that are now scattered across museums worldwide. Working with museum collections opens up possibilities for intersecting these subaltern interests and influences. This is more than just an exercise in inserting other voices; it reveals the nested colonialisms at work in the very infrastructures of disciplinary production that reach through to the present and influence how we speak about the past (Carruthers 2014).

1.2 Egypt, an Exotic Chronotope

The cross-cultural appeal of ancient Egypt is longstanding (Versluys 2020), but the museum is not simply a site for its popularization or for encounters with pre-existing facts. Examining an object from antiquity is never an unmediated connection to the past. Perceptions are informed by historical and social conditions, that in turn shape those conditions. When encountered in the museum some periods of an object's existence may be privileged over others, be that details of its production and use, its discovery and rediscovery, or its historic and contemporary interpretations from Afrocentrism to Science Fiction. Context is 'infinitely divisible and infinitely expandable' (Karp and Kratz 2014: 52), meaning that there are multiple temporalities for objects and all archaeological objects are polytemporal (Shalem 2012). Artefacts may attest to their own biographies, but they can also represent whole periods or cultures. They can be co-opted within narratives of change over long interludes of time or used to understand a single moment within it. Fundamentally, objects from the past exist in the present, as they have done in other presents. There can be, therefore, a tension between time as presented in linear historical sequences on the one hand and pasts that are co-present and overlapping on the other (Harris 2021). Can the multiplicity of times to which an object has belonged be effectively interwoven in academic interpretation and public display? Given the palimpsests that characterize Egyptian archaeology – from the Palaeolithic through to modern era in which sites, monuments, and artefacts were encountered, re-encountered, and transformed across millennia by different cultural, religious, and social groups – this becomes a tricky proposition.

Historical moments of meaning making, and how they are placed into dialogue with the present, are further contingent upon place. As a museum culture, ancient Egypt is a global phenomenon. Collections exist on every continent, apart from Antarctica, and in almost every country where local 'object habits' – that is the habituated attitudes to and practices around object engagements in a society or community generally – shape perceptions (Stevenson et al. 2017): in Brazil (Brancaglion 2018), China (Clarysse and

Yan 2006), Ghana (Morfini 2016), India (Bresciani and Betrò 2004), and central Asia (Hodjash 1995), to sketch just a few contours. Ancient Egyptian assemblages have also found a niche in multiple types of institution, including modern art galleries, ethnographic museums, and science centres. These positionalities are just one indication of the extraordinary breadth of relevancies of Egyptian collections, the multiple ways of knowing and realizing them, but also the potential for contesting them. Nevertheless, as Riggs (2013: 70) notes, the majority of museums today favour 'a presentation that avoids making temporal or geographic links with modernity', occluding the fact that modernity created those presentations.

'Ancient Egypt' remains one of the most popular subjects for temporary exhibitions worldwide (Shaya 2021). For many museum visitors, it constitutes a temporally collapsed 'time-space' or what could be called a 'chronotope', a term introduced by Russian literary scholar Bakhtin (1981) to describe how combinations of time and space are represented in language and discourse. Here, 'ancient Egypt' is considered a spatial–temporal whole, a particular type of setting made up variously of hieroglyphs, desert landscapes, riverine environments, mummies, pyramids, pharaohs, and antiquities, in which time, or more specifically the concept of 'ancient', 'thickens, takes on flesh, become[s] artistically viable' (Bakhtin 1981: 4). Collecting for, and displaying in, museums has had a large part to play in the creation of this chronotope. Things are valued because they are, paradoxically, timelessly old. Scholars are not immune to these ways of thinking as they share with museum professionals and publics a 'museal consciousness' (Crane 2000: 7).

This chronotope can further be characterized as being 'exotic', a term I use here in its anthropological sense not as something inherent to a place, time, or its objects, but as an aesthetic mode of perception that emerges from colonialism, 'a stimulating or exciting difference, something with which the domestic could be safely spiced' (Ashcroft et al. 2000: 94). Foster (1982) adds a further dimension presenting the exotic as dialectically functioning within a symbolic system, domesticating the foreign so that it is comprehensible yet defiant of total familiarity. And therein lies one of the challenges of addressing the colonial histories (and fantasies) that adhere to Egypt's objects regardless of their date; a resistance to the postcolonial imperative to demystify other cultures. It is why decolonization too has been unsettling for many, as it is seen to freight an antiquity of wonder and awe with modern baggage, thereby seemingly detracting from or disrupting that encounter. The problem is that awe and wonder are themselves subjective products of the 'specific historical, intellectual and even economic setting' of colonialism (Said 1978: 273) and tinged with imperial nostalgia (Fletcher 2012). How then can interpretive strategies be developed that both avoid exoticism and provide critical insights into the multiple times and places that constitute perceptions of Egyptian material while retaining a dialogue between those times rather than supplanting them? I suggest that multi-directional curation might be one means to achieve this.

1.3 Multi-Directional Curatorship

The project of assembling the variegated interpretive elements for museum objects – their records of acquisition, their archival ecosystems, and the places they operate in – often proceeds with reference to object biographies (Alberti 2005). It is a framework attentive to the shifting meanings and values of objects as they are continually recontextualized and brought into transformative relationships with people be they labourers, archaeologists, collectors, curators, conservators, or visitors. The model has been particularly productive for unfurling the numerous agencies that lie behind the formation of collections, including source communities that have been otherwise marginalized within heroic tales of Western discovery. One of the reasons for the prominence of the biographical approach to understanding museum objects is that it provides a compelling narrative hook (Alberti 2005: 561), a narrative being a communicative mode that conveys a succession of events within a temporal frame. However, as I will argue in Section 5 of this Element, rather than seeking to create linear biographies or fully fleshed stories, a multi-directional approach can encourage more nuanced life stories that foreground the fragmentary nature of archaeological knowledge, permitting alternative triangulations of time, place, and people simultaneously.

The idea derives from the work of Michael Rothberg (2009, 2014), whose concern has been the relationship between different social groups' histories of oppression and how they confront each other in the public sphere, in his case collective memories of Holocaust, colonialism, and slavery. Rothberg's work examines remembrances of the past and formations of identity in the present. He argues for a multi-directional memory in which, rather than different histories competing with each other, work 'productively through negotiation, cross-referencing, and borrowing' so that 'collective memories of seemingly distinct histories are not easily separable from each other, but emerge dialogically' (Rothberg 2014: 176). The past as a creation of the present infuses this study, and I suggest that multi-directionality might be a helpful framing device for subjects like Egyptology and archaeology which have multiple resonances for different publics, stakeholders, and scholars. Focussing on colonial histories in Egypt does not divert attention from understanding the ancient past, rather it demonstrates how these histories are implicated. Memory is the central theme of Rothberg's analysis, but it plays a more peripheral role in this discussion. My focus is a more general and looser leveraging of his concept towards the interpretation of the past in the present and the 'dynamic transfers that take place between diverse places and times' (Rothberg 2009: 11). In this project, I draw too from Max Silverman who notes that the layers that are created in this process capture 'the superimposition and productive interaction of different inscriptions and the spatialization of time' with the potential to offer 'a dynamic and open space composed of interconnecting traces of different voices, sites, and times' (Silverman 2013: 4).

The applicability of multi-directional memory to museums has been advanced by those working on histories of collection (Driver et al. 2021: 12), although how these might be implemented into museum practice has yet to be addressed. I raise the issue of public display and documentation in the context of the production of academic discourse because all museum work is fundamentally critical practice. As Moser (2008: 1050) notes, 'different types of non-academic discourse interact with academic ones in a complex and interdependent manner'. Exhibitions, along with cataloguing and database searches, can be recognized as forms of research experiment that have implications for insights into the past. Such a view aligns with developments in the history of science, which have collapsed distinctions between laboratories, field sites, and museums, underscoring how archaeological data evolve in its surrounds and is never fixed (Brusius 2017). Understanding museum formations and experimenting within them is a central part of how we think and know the past (see Section 5.2 for further development of these points).

2 Collecting Histories

It is increasingly recognized that Egyptologists 'continue to write our own history and not that of the ancient Egyptians' (Miniaci 2020: 414) through their projection of Western categories (Ambridge 2012; Lipson 2013), that the chronological structure for ancient Egypt was 'directly informed by the political state of affairs of the late nineteenth and early twentieth century' (Schneider 2008: 182), and that frameworks for interpreting ancient Egypt emerge less from the sources than from earlier deductive Victorian categories (Nyord 2018). Museums and their collections have been central to these projects and their examination affords the opportunity to interrogate those constructions. This section is therefore not meant to provide a history of discovery or an account of the acquisition of the collections Egyptologists work with today. Rather, it is an examination of how different sorts of historical narratives are themselves materially formed through collecting to represent knowledge claims. Modes of acquisition, together with the subsequent organization of collections, their documentation, and their display, all play a central role in the creation of disciplinary knowledge, including the definition of 'culture' (e.g. Kaplan 1995; Moser 2010). The practicalities of arranging collections did not just represent ancient cultures, rather they actualized the projection of European times and places onto them and in so doing became ingrained within the frameworks and the language that still underpins archaeological enquiry today. The imperative to understand collecting histories has further implications for morally accountable academic and museological practice, specifically in the context of the antiquities market through which Egyptian material continues to circulate, to which the last part of this section turns.

2.1 Periodization

How museums and their collections shape knowledge of the ancient past has varied throughout history. Hooper-Greenhill (1992), for example, in her explanation for how specific ideas around collections became validated at certain times, was influenced by Foucault's formulation of Renaissance, Classical, and Modern *epistemes* (systems of knowledge). For each of these historical eras, Foucault maintained, there existed distinctive *epistemes* that governed how people thought and formed discourse. Hooper-Greenhill extended this to the history of museums, arguing that systems of knowledge were materialized in the organization of collections. This is one means of viewing how ancient Egyptian artefacts were understood. In the Renaissance, Egyptian funerary figurines (shabtis) were frequently incorporated into the aesthetically and comparatively arranged sixteenth-century royal *Wunderkammer* and elite cabinets of curiosity, with little concern for date or provenance (MacGregor 2007: 180–3). During the Classical *episteme* of the late eighteenth and nineteenth centuries, taxonomic classificatory schemes situated Egyptian art as inferior to that of Greek art (Moser 2006). Within the Modern *episteme* of the later nineteenth-century public museum colonialism, imperialism, and nationalism informed audience receptions, new disciplinary structures, and 'civilizing' practices (for a more detailed overview across these centuries, see Riggs 2010).

Egyptian collections were largely amassed during the latter phase, constituting a distinctive 'antiquities rush' across the long nineteenth century (Marchand 2015). It involved several competing European countries, although the implications were not confined to Europe. Collecting was bound up with the formation of nation states further afield, such as Brazil, where the foundation of this newly independent state from Portugal in 1822 included the establishment of a National Museum with Egyptian antiquities at its core as a sign of imperial ambition (Funari and Funari 2010). Worldwide, collecting became entangled with the spread and professionalization of museum work, and the disciplinary establishment of new historical and fieldwork-based disciplines, including archaeology. At the centre of these new disciplines were objects, which through their physical presence and juxtapositions were deemed to provide irrefutable evidence for knowledge claims, what English archaeologist Flinders Petrie called 'material facts' (Stevenson 2019: 31). They could be proof of biblical times, testaments to the character of peoples, or demonstrations of the stage of a society's cultural attainment. These evidentiary needs suffused collection strategies and documentation, which requires understanding if modern research is to meaningfully engage with these assemblages.

New conceptions of time were produced across these centuries. As the Classical Age developed its systems of classification through archives, indexes, and filing systems, objects allowed time and change to be made manageable. Modernity further crystallized the reorganization of time as the world was rapidly transformed by industrialization, mechanization, and the extractive ideologies of colonialism. The narratives of progress that underpinned these developments produced new forms of historical consciousness that embraced ruins and antiquities, seeking to map them out along, but also to preserve them against, the march of time (Crane 2008: 101). A command of time not only became central to the production of art and culture, but also metonymically a form of control over Egypt and its peoples:

> The word *art* as it emerged in the mid- to late eighteenth century was linked to the imperial conquest and mastery of time, as if time were not something shared in common, but a divisible thing to be allocated. The mastering of time is a key aspect of imperial violence that separates the objects from people and places them in a progressive, linear timeline ('art history' is paradigmatic) in which colonized people and colonizers occupy different positions and roles. Under a unified idea of art, this image could be concretized in and through accumulated and displayed art objects. (Azoulay 2019: 60)

For Egyptian history this meant a hermetically sealed conception of pharaonic Egypt, dislocated from Egypt's modern inhabitants. Museums embodied this in their partitioning of pharaonic, classical, and Byzantine periods on the one hand, and Islamic pasts on the other, with the place of any given object with them often queried. Coptic objects, particularly, face contested categorization, variously being held in Roman, Byzantine/Medieval, or Egyptian departments (O'Connell 2014). Shatanawi (2021) offers a further example from the Netherlands, where taxonomic processes historically divided objects over the different museum disciplines of archaeology, art history, and ethnology, leading to a 'structural injustice' segregating Islamic cultures from pre-Islamic materials and implying degrees of inclusion and exclusion from Europe.

Contemporary material culture from groups such as the Fellahin (the Egyptian peasant class) has also been collected by archaeologists, but as examples of 'survivals' from ancient times (e.g. Blackman 1927; Figure 2). These actions were informed by Victorian social evolutionary theories whereby both ancient and modern objects were procured with the same end in mind: to demonstrate the technological characteristics relevant to the cultural 'age' of a society. This took precedence over their temporal location, casting 'primitive peoples' as survivals from a previous age into which they could give direct insight. It relegated modern Egyptians to a subordinate position within historical–cultural narratives regarding 'civilization', a logic Fabian (1983) termed 'allochronism'; a denial of coevalness. In this schema 'scientific' categorizations like 'savage' and 'civilized' reflected stages of historical development, with the 'civilized' West heir to the ancient civilization, and contemporary Egyptians an Orientalized East (Colla 2007: 103).

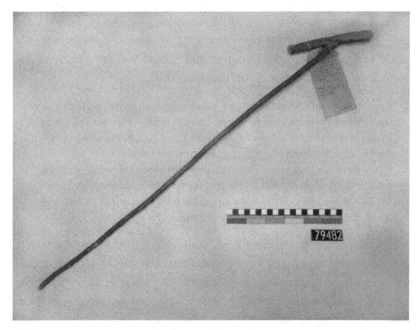

Figure 2 An example of an object acquired as a 'survival' from ancient Egypt. A wooden staff purchased by G. A. Wainwright in 1923 from 'Maaza Arabs, living on Eastern Desert of Egypt opposite Baliana' was thought to provide insight into ancient Egyptian *was*-sceptres. Courtesy of the Petrie Museum of Egyptian Archaeology (UC79482)

2.2 Acquisition Histories

The conditions under which collections have been acquired are of considerable importance for the twenty-first century museum, not to provide a processional celebratory historical narrative, but as a form of self-critique and public accountability. It was not the case that the extensive harvesting of antiquities for private collections and institutions were simply activities 'of their time', that Egyptians cared little for the heritage of their country, or that foreign protagonists acted out of benevolence to save antiquities, as common-place narratives have assumed. Egypt was not unregulated ground. The first antiquities laws covering Egypt were established by the Albanian-born and Turkish-speaking Ottoman Pasha, Muhammad Ali, through his 1835 *Antiqakhana* which strove to limit European removal of antiquities abroad and establish a national museum at Azbakeya, Cairo. The museum was short lived and his successor gave the collection away, splitting the assemblage between Istanbul and Austria. Nevertheless, further legislation developed over the decades and it is clear that tourists, military personnel, and diplomats were often fully aware of these prohibitions, however weakly enforced.

Price (2020: 224) gives the example of Manchester Museum donor Marianne Brocklehurst who described the 1873–1874 acquisition of a Third Intermediate Period mummy case in terms of adventure: 'we liked the idea of smuggling on a large scale under the nose of the Pasha's guards'. Meanwhile, Amelia Edwards, who can be lauded for her role in founding the Egypt Exploration Fund (EEF) and financing Petrie's career, confessed that collecting antiquities in Egypt (or the 'game' as she termed it) was 'prohibited, but we enjoyed it none the less because it was illegal. Perhaps we enjoyed it the more' (Edwards 1877: 449–50). Histories of collection too easily romanticize the appropriation of Egypt's heritage, but these examples highlight that narratives need to be more precise in the language used to characterize such activities. Often items in museums are recorded with donor details alongside a beneficent qualification such as 'gift of', a phrase that confers cultural capital onto those named, but abbreviating mechanisms of acquisition that were often more convoluted or morally questionable.

There was nothing inevitable about the export of antiquities and there were prominent voices of dissent (e.g. Pitt-Rivers 1882). Nevertheless, a system was established in 1883 that opened up the possibility for legally sanctioned excavations in Egypt and permissions to remove finds abroad. Known as 'partage', this system permitted export so long as the antiquities museum in Cairo had first choice of everything found. These new arrangements were the result of protracted negotiations between Petrie and the head of the French-run Antiquities

Service in Egypt, Gaston Maspero, on the impetus or pretence of museum needs (Stevenson 2019). Maspero's liberal approach to foreign exploration directly benefitted the museum in Cairo, which had a limited budget for mounting its own excavations to procure new collections: 'Musée s'est enrichi, sans bourse délier, d'une quantité de monuments précieux qu'il ne se serait pas procurés avec ses seules ressources' (Maspero 1912: XXX).[1] A decade later, these arrangements included the stipulation that concessions must involve a representative of Cairo's Egyptian Museum as part of the fieldwork team with the field director covering the expenses (Montserrat 1996: 166). For Petrie, museums were equally the underlying motivation for fieldwork:

> A specimen may be inferior to others already in a museum, and yet it will be worth more than all of them if it has its history; and it will be the necessary key, to be preserved with the better examples as a voucher of their historical position . . . .. The aim, then, in excavating should be to obtain and preserve such specimens in particular as may serve as keys to the collections already existing. (Petrie 1888: vii)

The emphasis on authenticity in this account was echoed by the director of the EEF's primary US beneficiary, the Boston Museum of Fine Arts, who noted that the objects received from the London-based organization meant that 'our Egyptian collection is thus being constantly strengthened by objects of which the authenticity is above all question' (Robinson 1903: 41). In Italy, Ernesto Schiaparelli was similarly minded. Although he has the reputation of establishing the newly unified Italian nation state's entry into the field of Egyptian archaeology through the foundation of the Italian Archaeological Mission in Egypt (MAI), the impetus was to fill gaps in the Turin Egyptian Museum. Excavation was seen by Schiaparelli as an alternative, cheaper means of collecting to purchasing objects from the art market, where the lack of certified provenance risked introducing forgeries into the collection (Jarsaillon 2017).

Other museums preferred to purchase from dealers where their emphasis was not necessarily authenticity, but completeness. In other words, timelessness, a desire to experience the past as if it had never elapsed. This was the case for the late nineteenth-century Danish National Museum in Copenhagen. In an 1899 letter written on behalf of its director, the curator Christian Blinkenberg explained to Egyptologist H.O. Lange that he wanted 'whole and complete pieces, no fragments of any kind' (cited in Hagen and Ryholt 2016: 24). Both of these impulses – to acquire the authentic and the complete – speak to the same aspiration: to have intimate and direct access to an object 'frozen in the moment

---

[1] 'The Museum has been enriched, without spending any money, with a large quantity of precious monuments that it would not have obtained with its own resources' (author's translation).

of their most emblematic value – of singularity, of implantation, and representativeness' (Crane 2008: 99).

Objects were thus validated by existing museum collections, becoming part of discursive formations (Foucault 1972), a reference to the ways in which collections are systematized with respect to each other and thereby shape discourse. In other words, circular reasoning; the museum configured artefacts into particular sets that pre-determined the types of material identified in the field as worth reporting and retaining. For instance, during excavations in the Fayum, which were principally focussed on recovering papyri and Fayum portraits, Egyptian teams 'found a few more things of interest', including 'locks, combs, &c &c [which] would be thankfully accepted, I know, by the Pitt Rivers Museum in Oxford' (letter from Hogarth dated 1896 cited in Montserrat 1996: 150). This was an a priori interest rather than one that addressed a research question or gave insight into the past. Locks had been one of Pitt-Rivers' earliest interests, which like his other object types, he arranged into sequences that demonstrated his politically conservative worldview of the gradual evolution (or degeneration) of culture from primitive to civilized (Pitt-Rivers 1883), in which vast spans of time and space could be comprehended at a glance.

These serial arrangements were influential not just throughout the museum world, but also in shaping what and how Egyptian material culture was interpreted. Take, for instance, Petrie's achievements in providing the first relative chronology of prehistoric remains – his Sequence Dating (SD) system of pottery from fourth-millennium BC Egypt, the Predynastic. It was indebted to Pitt-Rivers' arrangement of collections and it resonated with Petrie's own political worldviews (Sheppard 2010). In his article 'Sequences in Prehistoric Remains' Petrie (1899) reiterated the language of Pitt-Rivers, emphasizing the regularity of progression in the development of Predynastic material culture over time, despite the fact that his seriation method was an ordinal scale and not one that measured time in absolute years. This, therefore, was not merely a chronological framework, it was also an explanatory apparatus. Although explicit evolutionary explanations were largely abandoned over the course of the twentieth century, these nineteenth-century assumptions on how to organize collections remained entrenched within the language of Predynastic relative chronology and display, leading to continued reference by scholars to an unquestioned slow, gradual development of the Egyptian state, with temporal subdivisions of the Predynastic of equal length (e.g. Hoffman 1979; Savage 2001). Only recently have these been challenged by statistically modelled radiocarbon dates and which demonstrate the variable lengths of these periods in absolute years, a project wholly based on organic samples from museum collections (Stevenson 2015b).

The nature of collections, their methods and histories of acquisition, influenced the types of knowledge produced about ancient Egypt in several other ways, some more subtly than others. An example is one of the most ubiquitous categories of Egyptian artefact held by institutions worldwide; shabtis. Despite their omnipresence they have played a limited role in scholarship (Howley 2020; Nyord 2018). The lack of serious critical attention given to them is partly a corollary of their popularity amongst private collectors, with museum curators historically dismissive of their value (Howley 2020: 126–7). Their multitudes have afforded largely typological studies and numerous catalogues of museum collections, albeit with limited contextual interrogation. They nevertheless remain staple features not only of permanent museum display (Figure 3), but also in museum outreach and educational programmes where conventional narratives of their role in taking on the burdens of *corvée* labour in the afterlife are repeated without question. As Nyord (2018: 75) comments, these modern contexts of interpretation privilege 'simple, univocal and immediately understandable explanation ... as opposed to one requiring relatively detailed discussions of archaeological contexts and textual transmission'. Arguably both publics and scholars share a museal consciousness whereby shabtis are so commonplace as to require little explication.

A second consequence of shabtis' collectability was the creation of forgeries to meet demand. So desired were they that playful recreations and fabrications were already being produced by the mid-seventeenth century (Whitehouse 1989). And these were not rare. By the end of the eighteenth century, the taste for Egyptian-style pieces prompted the creation of numerous high-quality forgeries of sculptures and metalwork. These now 200-year-old productions abound in museum collections and have been routinely published by leading scholars (Lilyquist 1988: 32–7). This becomes particularly complex for interpreting the past when provenances are attributed to forgeries by dealers and mixed with artefacts that are genuinely from Egyptian antiquity. One such example is a series of artefacts that emerged on the market in 1916 which were purported to be part of the tomb of pharaoh Thutmose III's wives. Most were purchased by the Met and published by its curator Henry Winlock in 1948. The assemblage became part of heated debates on the nature of harem life in New Kingdom Egypt, although framed largely in terms of the gendered expectations of the twentieth century (Wilfong 2010: 172). Lilyquist's (2003) analysis of the tomb's associated documentation revealed that up to a third of the material attributed to the burials were modern forgeries. A further complicating dimension was the practice of paying *bakhshish* to Egyptian excavators on archaeological digs, extra being given for notable discoveries. Ostensibly, this was to ensure finds were handed to the foreign expedition leaders rather than

Figure 3 Display of shabtis in the UCL Petrie Museum of Egyptian
Archaeology, London. © Alice Stevenson

local dealers. In reality, it often had the effect of introducing forgeries directly
into the ground, where they became part of the season's documented finds (e.g.
Adams 1993).

These are just some of the complexities that those studying collections today
need to be aware of. A naïve reliance on a particular excavator's reputation,
such as Petrie's lionization as purveyor of scientific method, should not be taken

as a vector of provenience certainty. Almost all early archaeologists purchased material for museums in addition to fieldwork. The prevalence of forgeries has had, however, a secondary effect upon knowledge construction in giving rise to a form of 'counter-expertise' (Kaeser 2011). To distinguish 'real' from 'fake' required greater attention to ancient technologies, to find evidence for production and consumption. This has led to greater investment in analytical evaluation of the physical and chemical properties of artefacts, themselves of broader interest for understanding ancient societies. Recent work employing Reflectance Transformation Imaging to identify tool marks on stone is one example. Largely introduced to identify authentic artefacts, it now provides valuable insight into ancient techniques and skills, allowing reconstructions of the tools used to make such marks (Serotta 2014). Forgeries are also a useful mirror to contemporary values and the creation of archaeological imaginaries, themselves a rich subject of scholarly study and exhibition (Schoske and Wildung 1983).

Partage itself profoundly shaped the composition and research potential of collections. The system was of enormous benefit to British archaeological enterprises who, in the absence of government grants, secured financial support through a transnational network of institutional and private funding that had the explicit goal of furnishing museums worldwide with finds. It led to a symbiotic dependency between museums and fieldwork with institutional demands affecting the type of site excavated (preferably funerary contexts) and the profile of artefacts available for study. Single excavation seasons are now dispersed to multiple locations, sometimes continents apart, posing considerable obstacles for researchers navigating dissimilar cataloguing systems and administrative structures (Stevenson 2019). Once finds are located and cross-referenced the picture produced is but a partial reflection of what was originally unearthed.

Franzmeier (2021) discusses in detail the direct effects of museum collecting strategies on the publication and construction of knowledge from the 1920 to 1921 archaeological work at Sedment led by Petrie. Much of the excavation report was produced post-season back in London in consultation with the select objects that had been permitted for export through partage. The publication, the observations and inferences drawn therein, was therefore skewed towards material deemed to be suitable for museums. And museums were primarily only interested in objects of certain periods. Thus, from Sedment the much-desired material from 1520 BC to 1075 BC (New Kingdom) is over-represented in both the publication (Petrie and Brunton 1924) and in museum collections, while post-New Kingdom material is largely missing. Even though Petrie had an interest in the opening centuries of the first millennium BC, little of the materials found at Sedment belonging to this time period were published or presented to museums. Through these processes, periodizations, and what is considered representative, became more rigidly defined and harder to challenge. The implications of partage have methodological significance for contemporary research since museum acquisitions were a cornerstone for the creation of typologies in the nineteenth and early twentieth centuries. The coincidence of archaeological development and partage has led to particular artefacts to become considered 'standard' over-cited examples that all future excavated material is evaluated relative to. Boozer (2015) noted this with reference to domestic archaeology of Roman Egypt. Its preeminent exemplar is a structure at Karanis in the Fayum, collections from which are held by the University of Michigan's Kelsey Museum. Numerous specialist publications have been produced, focussing on material categories prioritized in the museum rather than with reference to original archaeological contexts. The individualizing nature of these presentations – realized and reified by museum practices – she argues, can lead to a 'tyranny of typologies', whereby systems that seek to create order and sequence to reveal patterns in the past, in actual fact conceal difference. Typological analysis both stretches data and provides it with a visual focus which holds attention on specific examples so frequently that ambiguous outliers may be ignored: 'Over time, scholars begin to limit their analytical spectrum and confuse dominant images with reality' (Boozer 2015: 97).

Exhibition catalogues and museum displays, which often only showcase a small percentage of their stored collections,[2] contribute significantly to the construction of what is 'typical' of the past. In turn, this can determine how emerging data are defined and what counts as evidence. Particularly problematic are unique and singular items where there is no, or else limited, comparative material, yet which become elevated through repeated citation to represent larger categories of evidence. One example is a limestone figurine of woman with a pot in the Petrie Museum (Figure 4). As the only known representation of a female engaged in what has been interpreted to be pottery production, long considered a male-only domain, it has been included without critical reflection in high-profile exhibitions (e.g. Capel and Markoe 1996: 15), and subsequently cited in reference works on the ancient world (Harrington 2018: 546). The artefact, however, is unprovenanced, having been purchased by Petrie sometime before 1915. Without archaeological context, not only should its authenticity be questioned but so too should its representativeness of ancient practices. Yet it is its recent association with Petrie, rather than any ancient one, that is taken as an indicator of authority and

---

[2] The extent of display is frequently dependent upon institution or collection size. In some institutions, such as the Met or the archaeological museum in Trieste, Italy, the majority of the holdings are exhibited.

Figure 4 An unprovenanced figurine of a woman and a pot purchased by Flinders Petrie on display in the UCL Petrie Museum of Egyptian Archaeology, London. UC15706. © Alice Stevenson

significance. In an incomplete past, where ancient identities may be frustratingly elusive, present-day projections too easily fill the gaps.

To maintain these values of singularity and representativity, museums have not only been selective in what they have acquired, but they have also been discriminatory in what they have displayed and retained, as this account from a 1950s re-display in the Brooklyn Museum attests, in which the curators sought to:

'. . . eliminate the dreary, crumbling rubbish from ancient cemeteries which inexplicably finds place in the Egyptian departments of many museums and which can only give a distorted idea of Egyptian civilization' (Riefstahl 1953: 31).

More drastic still was disposal, a readily used tool of collection development, like the British Museum's destruction of iron tools from Naukratis in the late 1880s (Stevenson 2019: 35), the Brooklyn Museum's sale of parts of de Morgan's fieldwork in their gift shop in 1959 (Meleounis 2009: 15), and Toledo Museum of Art's disposal by public auction of elements of its founding collection in 2016 (Dawson 2016). Museums are more porous than many people realize.

All of the above leads to rather pessimistic views of the potential of museum collections for meaningful archaeological analysis. But critical scrutiny of legacy assemblages can be generative of fresh interpretations and while retrieval of old data may involve considerable efforts in understanding histories, assessing it can potentially destabilize long-established evidential claims (Chapman and Wiley 2016: 95–96). Stored museum collections can themselves challenge 'the tyranny of typology' since no one site can individually provide insight into a society or time period. As Robins (2008: 12) notes 'visit any museum's reserve collections or examine the finds from many an excavation in Egypt, and you will discover another world completely'. While archaeologists may prefer to work with freshly excavated material, constructing a dichotomy between field and museum is unhelpful (Whitley 2016). More productive is to put legacy data into dialogue with related collections, fresh fieldwork, and scientific techniques, such as the innovative work in the Fayum region re-examining Neolithic sites first recorded by Caton-Thompson and Gardener (Holdaway et al. 2022). Here the team has established relationships between different datasets: artefacts in museums, observations on objects resting on the present-day field surface, satellite imagery, and sediment analysis. Using a bespoke data management system, they were able to add metadata and spatial references to different attributes, allowing the incorporation of both legacy and new fieldwork findings to exist within one framework. The approach deliberately tries to move beyond typologically based, culture-historical reconstruction towards a more dynamic relocation of artefacts within the landscapes in which they were found and the people they have historically been associated with.

2.3 Documenting Histories

Once artefacts cross a museum's threshold they are transformed through acts of registration (accessioning),[3] object marking, and cataloguing which all seek to

---

[3] Accessioning is the formal commitment by museums to care for objects in the long term. It differs from museum acquisition whereby a museum acquires legal title to an object but may not formally accession it into its collection. Once an object is accessioned it is subject to strict museum policies regarding care and use, and it is not easily disposed of without following strict protocols.

stabilize and institutionalize culturally significant categories (Jenkins 1994: 257). Documentation can have profound repercussions for how material is understood, as objects and bodies are assigned to particular sub-collections through numbering regimes and words become sedimented within information infrastructures. Cross-referencing through these archival inscriptions may reveal details that have larger historical implications, while research into the minutiae of numbering systems can have repercussions for understanding the ancient past. Manuelian (2015), for instance, documented a series of numbering misidentifications and re-identifications on excavation notecards in the Giza archives held by the Boston Museum of Fine Arts, which provided persuasive evidence with regard to the debate on whether Old Kingdom false doors or slab stela were the focus of cult activity. Riggs (2016), meanwhile, has examined the archival processes through which human remains have become museum specimens. In her example from Manchester Museum, the inscription of catalogue numbers ensured that a 5,000-year old skeleton from Abydos was assigned to the ethnographic rather than Egyptological collection in the 1920s, a move betraying the assumptions that separated 'science' from 'art', including those relating to racial science.

Beyond the significance of the ancient artefact itself then are the important traces of the engagements of curators, excavators, and researchers left upon them; labels, stickers, pen marks, and incisions (Figure 5). Labelling or numbering an artefact is an essential collections management task to avoid dissociation between an object and information about it. Coote (2012: 13) notes, however, that writing on a museum object may also be seen as constituting an essential truth about it, be that its date or locale. Indeed, the dates and site names inked, etched, or stamped onto Egyptian material can too readily provide leading interpretive assumptions about that object. For example, many site names have become a shorthand for wider regions or periods of time; Badari and Naqada have become indexical for the Predynastic period, Lahun the Middle Kingdom, and Deir el-Medina the New Kingdom. Yet all of these sites demonstrate centuries and millennia of activity, as well as topographically diverse, expansive landscapes. One of the reasons for this reductive approach to site perception is that another underlying motivation for inscribing excavated artefacts with site names or codes was to authenticate their place in museum sequences of objects, in other words to as act more as temporal than spatial references (e.g. Petrie 1888: vii), and this has become a primary axis of archaeological interpretation. This way of treating site names has led to numerous misidentifications (e.g. Figure 6). Such loss of precision in archaeological context, trumped by the needs of sequence over site, has implications for contemporary interpretations of the past.

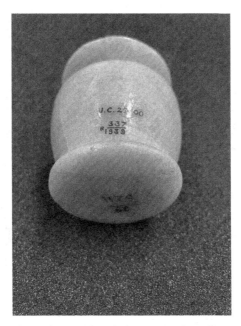

Figure 5 An Egyptian kohl vessel with three sets of numbers on it. UC25500 is the Petrie Museum registration (accession number) written in the late twentieth century on a layer of paraloid B72 so that it can be removed if needs be. An earlier mark, R337/1939, has been directly inked onto the object and is the number given to it by the Wellcome Museum which originally held the object before its transfer to the Petrie Museum. Earlier still, is the number 29/5211, an excavation mark added in 1929 and relating to the object to a tomb excavated at Mostagedda

The act of labelling extends objects into relations with other documents, where the associated terminology, and its interpretive implications, echoes across from the past to the present. Ink inscriptions on objects and accession registers are transcribed onto index card catalogues, which are then typed into museum content management systems, and subsequently made publicly visible in online search engines. Consequently, contemporary databases, imbued with their historical legacies, become sites for the re-performance of authoritative colonial-era collecting and modes of thought (Turner 2020). As Phillips (2011: 95) has argued for ethnographic museums, there is an 'intimate connection between naming and power', allowing European terms, language, and points of reference to entirely frame Egyptian heritage and emphasizing the object in the museum rather than in the context of the archaeological site.

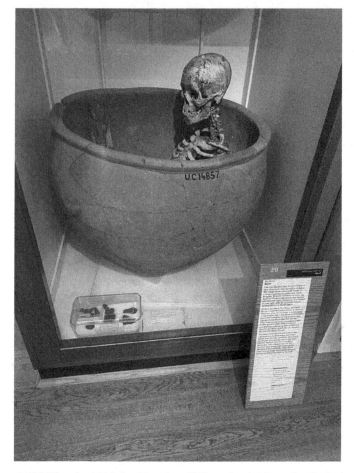

Figure 6 Old Kingdom (third millennium BC) pot burial from the Badari region in the Petrie Museum of Archaeology, often incorrectly attributed to the Predynastic period (© Alice Stevenson)

This sort of legacy data is found in all museums, adhering to its objects. These are not neutral descriptors, since naming conventions are interpretive acts that are historically situated and culturally constructed. For example, 'soul-house' is a common category of artefact in museum catalogues, perpetuating a nomenclature imposed by Petrie from anthropological comparisons with African 'soul huts' and Jewish customs. There is no interpretive support for such comparisons and the name ultimately misrepresents their possible functions. Even outdated references to obscure items like 'tip-cats' – a popular English Victorian toy, but one that few would recognize in the twenty-first century – remain in museum registers imposing not just a specious functional identity onto enigmatic pieces of wood, but also a worldview that saw Victorian London taken as a model for an archaeological imagining of the second millennium BC Egyptian settlement of Lahun (Petrie 1890: 30). These designations preserve old interpretations, inflecting constantly on current discourse that has to work hard against them.

The accessibility of collections to the public and researchers is also conditioned by cataloguing infrastructures, which may require expertise in order to search and retrieve documented artefacts. Language barriers are particularly acute in Egypt itself, where the documentation of collections in Cairo is complex, reflecting its nested colonial history and inequities in resource allocation (Rashed and Bdr-El-Din 2018). In the Egyptian Museum in Cairo, the *Journal d'Entrée* has been the primary registration system since the 1880s, although it is complemented by a thematic catalogue, the *Catalogue général du Musée du Cairo*, and a *Temporary Register*. Throughout, entries are variously written only in French, others exclusively in English, while more recently Arabic has also been used. New initiatives, such as the US-funded 'Egyptian Museum Database Project', an internal rather than publicly-facing collections management system, are guided by documentation systems written only in English.[4] While the twenty-first century has seen moves towards 'Arabising' sciences, it remains almost exclusively *fusha* (Classical Arabic), one that is highly academic, written rather than spoken.

Equally problematic, is the uncritical repetition of racist, colonialist, and ableist nomenclature. One colonialist term still commonly encountered in Egyptology, as well as on online museum databases, is the word 'pygmy'. It has been used historically in anthropology to refer to diverse peoples of short stature, usually those from Equatorial Africa or parts of Asia, and has been applied more recently in several countries as an insult in reference to a person's intellectual abilities. It is a term that has been explicitly identified as one that museums should avoid (Modest and Lelijveld 2018: 133), not just because of its pejorative connotations, but also because it lumps together different peoples under a single category that holds unhelpful colonial baggage suggesting cultural relatedness (Robillard and Bahuchet 2012). Such terms should be subject to review, not erased from information management systems, but rather de-centred, contextualized, and historicized accordingly. For example, anti-Semitic conventions regarding appearance were applied to terracotta heads from Ptolemaic Egypt in the Petrie Museum (e.g. UC33278), but now have

---

[4] But see the *Eternal Egypt* project which is multilingual including Arabic: www.eternalegypt.org/ EternalEgyptWebsiteWeb/HomeServlet?page.refresh=Y&ee_website_action_key=action.display .home&language_id=1&new_language_id=3

detailed catalogue entries, based on discussions with Jewish communities, as to why the term is problematic (Challis 2013: 129–32).

Databases are of concern as they are not merely information repositories, but tools in the further production of knowledge as researchers experiment with searches. Cataloguing structures prioritize and limit information recorded about artefacts often reducing material to a common set of properties (type, material, date). Accession registers and card catalogues provide only limited space leading to abbreviated collections histories, while databases impose syntax controls on singular fields. As attention is increasingly paid to the multiple agencies behind archaeological discoveries (Mickel 2021; Quirke 2010), how information infrastructures accommodate new identifications should be considered to allow for the assembly of multi-directional histories. This may mean repeating fields within museum databases for 'collector' or 'place', as well as special fields for 'old descriptions' or 'histories of interpretation', but also being open to contemporary Egyptian terms and definitions.

Such actions are not simply demonstrations of 'political correctness'. They are an explicit recognition of how terms like this have functioned in societal discourses and power dynamics to racially demean and disempower, as well as an acknowledgement that these more recent histories cannot be detached from how the past is perceived and understood. To draw attention to these words signals a more self-reflexive mode of interpretation – what in archival circles is referred to as 'conscientious description' – sensitive to how different people relate to these multiple pasts in the present and to the institutions and professionals that represent it. Museum databases act as vital structures for institutional memory, but they should not go unchallenged. The labour and resources required to address museum documentation, however, are considerable when collection items number upwards in the thousands, even hundreds of thousands. Moreover, these are not just technical projects, but research ones working against the archival grain. New priorities for collections management must, therefore, be set on par with curatorial agendas so that they become more central to the disciplinary production of knowledge, not just a tool in its service.

2.4 The Antiquities Market

Artefacts have not been allowed to leave Egypt since 1983 and the passing of Law 117. However, the Egyptian Ministry of Tourism and Antiquities, and most museums when undertaking due diligence on the provenance of material prior to a new acquisition, accede to the date 1970. This is the year in which the UNESCO Convention on the Means of Prohibiting and Preventing the Illicit Import, Export, and Transfer of Ownership of Cultural Property was established. Subsequently, 1970 has come to delineate a shift in museum practices from the period before the Convention, when illicit trafficking and looting were either not understood or deemed unimportant, to the period after, when these issues became more widely acknowledged across the sector. Most acquisition policies therefore use 1970 as a normative threshold (Gerstenblith 2019). Yet the Convention should not simply be seen as a convenient means of distinguishing between 'good' and 'bad' antiquities, and it should not lead to abbreviated investigations acquisition histories (MacKenzie et al. 2019: 97–8). Indeed, the ICOM maintains that due diligence 'should establish the full history of the item since discovery or production' (ICOM 2017 article 2.3).

Looted artefacts, nonetheless, continue to find their way into foreign institutions as the desire for timeless art transcends the needs of provenance. Market actors, it is argued, are still to this day more concerned with establishing authenticity than verifiable collection histories (MacKenzie et al. 2019). The latter, however, is frustrated by false provenance, fraudulent paperwork, and irregularities in transnational export regulations. The first of these is facilitated by colonial histories, with a common tactic being to attribute artefacts to 'old English ownership', as was the case for a 3,500-year-old mural from the tomb of Sobekhotep in Luxor which was removed illegally around 1980 and found its way to the University of Bonn (Wessel 2015: 6–7). On 15 February 2019, meanwhile, the Metropolitan Museum of Art issued a press statement detailing its return of a first century BC coffin to Egypt having learned that its ownership history and associated documentation had been forged. Evidence demonstrated it had been looted from Egypt in 2011, but although associated with a period of disruption following the Arab Spring, this was not a causative reason for the theft. Antiquities torn from their contexts travel along pre-existing channels not created by war or civil unrest but pulled through currents of demand from rich market countries (Parcak et al. 2016). Simply tackling looting in source countries alone without addressing the demand end of the antiquities trade is ultimately misguided. The Antiquities Trafficking and Heritage Anthropology Research (ATHAR) project, for instance, has drawn attention to social media's role as a significant platform on which prominent auction houses' sales prices are shared as a means of highlighting market interest to organized criminal gangs who can loot to order. It demonstrates a clear link between demand in economically dominant countries and its impact on those with less resources (Al-Azm and Paul 2019).

While the destruction of heritage invites international condemnation, with archaeological rhetoric quick to lament the loss of contextual information imperative for meaningful interpretation of the past, this should not be the only consequence recognized; there are humanitarian implications as much as professional ones. Site guards have been murdered by criminal gangs intent on looting, children have died after being impelled to tunnel for antiquities, and many have been injured during clandestine excavations, all to feed market demand outside of Egypt (Hanna 2016). These injuries are most likely to be sustained by those who exist in extreme poverty, leading to their identification as 'subsistence looters', people who are paid a tiny fraction of the final market sale for antiquities. They take the biggest risks, for the lowest return.

Understanding and being transparent about the history of collections is not just the responsibility of museums. It is also a vital skill for academics as well since the trade in antiquities relies upon expertise to validate material (Brodie 2017). For these reasons, many professional organizations and institutions ask that their members do not publish material whose provenance prior to 1970 is not clear. Even prior to this date museums and academics can make efforts to normalize language around context that more explicitly acknowledges the circumstances of an 'acquisition', whether it is purchased, for instance, and whether its provenance is known. To do so, would encourage a more ethically minded practice that acknowledges that the quest for access to the past is not just informed by the present, but has consequences within it.

3 Materials

One of the c.80,000 index cards held in the Petrie Museum documents a fragmentary ivory Predynastic figurine registered under number UC4253 (Figure 7). The record provides not just a concise classification of the artefact, but also a series of reference points to dates and locations – the tomb number it was found in at Naqada (271), the 'sequence date' it was attributed to (S.D. 38), and the publications that it has featured in. Later annotations, inked in pen, codify another archival location, namely the catalogue number for the photograph (E.Neg.338 (group1)), a print of which adheres to the card. Stamped in red at the top right-hand corner is the word 'TREATED', an indication that the artefact has been subject to conservation, although details of the intervention are not given. They may perhaps exist in a separate file, under a unique conservation number. Pencil marks cross out a measurement in inches, leaving the addition of a measurement in centimetres, while a coating of white correction fluid clarifies a publication page citation. The document highlights how every museum object exists in an ecosystem of archival locations (Jones 2021), accruing new interpretations over time. But it also reveals the prior knowledge that is required to translate, understand, and locate relevant information, details usually reserved for a small number of professionals.

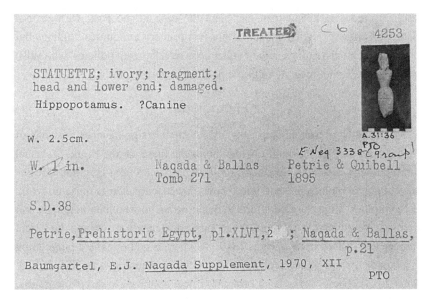

Figure 7 Index card for UC4253, a fourth millennium BC ivory statuette,
excavated in Egypt by Flinders Petrie's teams now in UCL Petrie Museum of
Egyptian Archaeology. © Alice Stevenson

The parallel histories of museum and archival professionalization have often
led to a separation of objects from associated documentation that might con-
textualize them (Jones 2021). For instance, archives relating to the Museo
Egizio Turin are held in the State Archive not the museum, meaning that
focussed research efforts are needed to reconnect lost histories (Cafici 2021).
It is a situation called 'dissociation', one of ten agents of deterioration that
adversely affects museum collections. Consequently, research with museum
collections frequently involves extensive archival study in order to reconnect
disparate pieces of information. But these fragments of evidence are not ancil-
lary to the archaeological object; the attendant practices of field recording,
conservation, and interpretation are often key components in its creation.
These products of fieldwork may equally find space in museums and archival
institutions, where additional treatments further shape their potential. These are
objects of critical reflection in their own right with different material properties
and histories, but they are not always catalogued or accessible.

A multi-directional approach to collection interpretation therefore needs to
be attentive to archival documents – be they photographs, casts, models, or
conservation records – as the antiquities that museums steward, not least
because archives may be used for purposes quite different to those envisaged
by those who established them. The twenty-first century museum takes these

resources more seriously than has been the case in the past, with several institutions now explicitly including not just primary antiquities holdings but also their archival holdings in their collections development policies, while also creating systems to integrate multiple points of reference for any single item.

3.1 Photographs

A robust body of scholarship now exists on the significance and role of photographs within museums. Chief amongst these is the work of visual anthropologist Elizabeth Edwards (2010), who has brought attention not just to what photographs represent, but to how they function across museum work. In Egyptology, Riggs has led efforts to demonstrate how both photography and archives are 'dynamic participants in our understanding of both historical practice and history itself' (Riggs 2019: 8). There is additionally a burgeoning scholarship on how photography operates within archaeology (e.g. Baird 2020; Guha 2013). These works have brought critical appraisal to the photographic collections that have a substantial presence in the backrooms of institutions, but a more limited visibility in museum documentation and public profiles.

In the Petrie Museum, London, six large metal filing cases contain more than 1,000 heavy, fragile glass plate negatives relating to fieldwork led by Petrie (Picton and Pridden 2008; Quirke 2009), amidst a larger archive of nearly 7,000 negatives, prints, and albums. In the Kelsey Museum of Archaeology, Michigan, are some 8,000 negatives from the 1920 excavations at Karanis (Wilfong 2012), while more recently, the Royal Museums of Art and History in Brussels, has sought to make more accessible the photographic collection of 7,000 glass negatives (Claes et al. 2021). The increased attention given to these types of collections in the twenty-first century is partly a product of their materiality; their flat, square, or rectangular profiles lend themselves to reproductive technologies like flatbed scanners (Edwards and Morton 2015: 18). Digitization seems a quick solution to bulky, delicate, and otherwise inaccessible media. But like any other collection they demand research to provide appropriate metadata in order to facilitate record retrieval.

While these aforementioned collections are material products of excavation, almost all museums additionally house photographic assemblages made as result of institutional operations; conservation, collections management, marketing, and education which rely on visual representations of artefacts. Consequently, photographs in the museum, Edwards (2019) observes, may be both collections (as significant objects in their own right subject to cataloguing, policy development, and care) and non-collections (as a management and communication tool). Taken together, the volume of photographic resources held by museums is significant. Yet rarely do these collections find a significant place within galleries or displays, with some rare exceptions in mostly temporary exhibitions (e.g. Del Vesco and Moiso 2017). Treated as images, these collections have primarily been used as useful, albeit unproblematized data source for Egyptologists attempting to re-establish finds contexts and conditions of recovery. Regarded, as material culture that is collected and curated, they form a resource that can be read 'against the grain', to reveal the interpretive strategies of disciplines, situated within colonial contexts that enabled Egyptian archaeology. It is a means to develop more holistic narratives regarding the multiple agencies involved in archaeological projects, inclusive of Egyptian communities (Riggs 2017b), like Mohammedani Ibrahim, a site photographer whose name was written on thousands of photographic prints associated with Reisner's excavations yet cropped out of publications (Wray 2021).

Photographic resources in museums have been subject to a variety of inscriptional practices. They may have been mounted, numbered, cut, coloured, or annotated, ensuring that they are always tethered to the contexts of institutional time and its histories. Petrie's *Aims and Methods in Archaeology* advised, for instance, that when setting up objects for photography in the field that less significant examples be placed at the periphery of the camera's field of vision, so that they could be cropped out for publication if deemed necessary (Petrie 1904: 81). The photographic archive sometimes bears the physical traces of these decisions in the traces of sticky tape residue, pencil marks, and other annotations. By these means artefacts were extracted from field sites into new contexts of archaeological interpretation (Klamm 2015: 47–51). Silences in the archive have also been produced as early field negatives on cellulose nitrate have been disposed of on account of their combustibility. In such processes the negatives may have been scanned or copied, but the original material properties or annotations are not always recorded as the photographic object is too easily reduced to image.

When photographs are featured in permanent galleries, they are further manipulated in specific ways. Edwards and Lien (2014), for example, have considered how photographs may be used as 'evidentiary ballast', a design solution that creates an ambience rather than providing specific information or as a basis for direct interpretive efforts. This includes generic, background photomurals of Egyptian landscapes writ large upon gallery walls – typically the pyramids at Giza, feluccas on the Nile, or the temples at Luxor (Figure 8). When photomurals extend to the edges of walls and are left uncaptioned, they may suggest an undifferentiated 'past time'. Notably, these are images usually either commissioned or purchased from picture libraries rather than drawn from

Figure 8 Photomurals of Egyptian landscapes used in the ancient Egyptian gallery at the National Museum of Scotland in February 2019. © Paige Brevick

the museum's own archive, selected by designers rather than curators. Moreover, the environments depicted are static, devoid of the modern peoples that today live amidst those spaces, cropping out, for example, the urban expanse of Cairo from the Giza plateau so as to leave intact an imagined Egypt, isolated from the here and now:

> This emptiness, however, is occupied by the viewer's imagination of what can be reconstructed within its bounds, positioning the present absence in a way that invites our consideration of its past. The photograph is something like a stage set in which archaeological vision can be acted out (Bohrer 2011: 11).

Where Egyptological archives are drawn upon to illustrate the archaeological context of displayed finds, the image itself may equally provide drama and atmosphere when inflated to fill a wall space or as a backdrop to a display case (Figure 9). Such a strategy allows photographs to 'expand the object beyond the case into an impression of lived experience' (Edwards and Lien 2014: 8). In these cases that lived experience is arguably a more recent past rather than an ancient one. The sepia tones, monochrome images, and greyscale prints of these reproductions are evocative of an affective 'past' (Edwards 2010: 31) that may not lead the viewer to immediately consider ancient times, but rather elicit

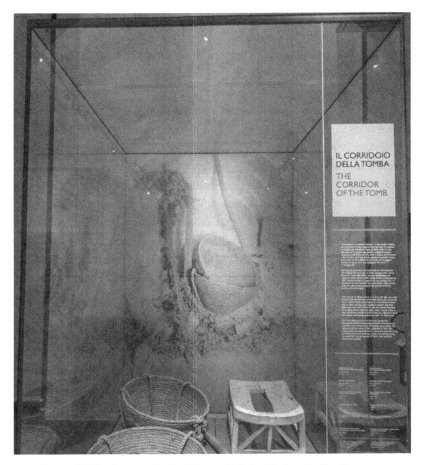

Figure 9 Display case in the Museo Egizio, Turin. © Alice Stevenson

colonial nostalgia for a 'golden age' of discovery in the early twentieth century when such black and white photographs were the norm (Riggs 2020: 198). Photographic manipulation Riggs (2019: 38) argues can also present a particular archaeological aesthetic for the 'untouched' past. A case in point is the antechamber of Tutankhamun's tomb in which the interventions of the fieldwork – the electric lights, wires, and scales – were moved or cropped out of sight for Harry Burton's photographic documentation.

These are not just issues for the museum professional. Academics equally draw from these photographic collections to provide visual content for their research papers, scholarly tomes, and coffee-table books. One form of publication that has significant intellectual currency in Egyptology, and which provides certain styles of collection encounter and camerawork, is the exhibition catalogue. Nineteenth-century catalogues tended simply to be pamphlets, listing objects and their dates, but have evolved to include substantial visual content, critical essays, and bibliographies. These are no longer guides to be carried around galleries, but rather are purchased after visiting, or indeed as a proxy for attending, an exhibition. Their glossy heft exudes authority, the objects brought together certified by institutional prestige. These edited volumes transcend the transience of a curated show through publication and circulation, becoming frequently cited works in their own right (e.g. Bourriau and Quirke 1988; Capel and Markoe 1996; Russman 2001). The photographic treatments inside generally individualize each object; they are set against a neutral backdrop, positioned without a scale, and carefully orientated so that any modern markings on the objects – museum registration numbers, excavator's context codes, or collector's cataloguing notations – are obscured from view, all emphasizing their status as timeless *objets d'art* rather than archaeological or museological artefacts (Baird 2020: 85; Riggs 2019: 113), while additionally situating them within a globalized phenomenon of art consumption (Joyeux-Prunel and Marcel 2015).

These processes of decontextualization have a long history in archaeology (Figure 10). The lack of archaeological context further allows unexcavated material, illicit artefacts, and modern forgeries to occupy the same space as excavated finds, where they share confidently attributed typological and chronological credentials, skirting over their lack of provenance, and permitting their inclusion into canon. This practice of individualization, an effect also produced in display, further emphasizes the rare, the complete, and the unusual, creating a false perception of the archaeological record and contributing to the 'tyranny of typologies' (as per 2.2).

3.2 Replicas

Photographs constitute one technology in a continuum of complementary forms of reproduction (Barker 2010). Plaster casts, electrotypes, rubbings, and squeezes were a significant focus for museums and international fairs throughout the nineteenth and early twentieth centuries. They were an alternative modality of collecting that contributed towards the creation of canon, enhanced the fame of individual artefacts, bolstered the prestige of institutions holding originals, and permitted those outside of Egypt to maintain intellectual authority over material that could not or was not permitted to leave the country. In many cases, such objects have been central to the establishment of Egyptology, part of a strategy of authenticating knowledge. The Rosetta Stone, for instance, is amongst the most reproduced of all Egyptological artefacts, with the first copies made by French lithographers just a year after it was seized in 1799 by

Figure 10 A photograph of statue excavated during the Egypt Exploration Fund's work at Abydos in 1910 with a backdrop held up by an unnamed Egyptian worker (EES archive image number AB.NEG.10.115). Courtesy of the Egypt Exploration Society

Napoleon's army. Together with plaster casts, these imprints circulated widely throughout Europe, with intellectuals such as Champollion largely working from copies (Regulski 2018). The stone's surface was repeatedly subjected to episodes of inking, sulphur and plaster casting, wax coatings, and charcoal rubbings.

Traditions of replication have varied globally, with different knowledge cultures approaching Egyptian material within their own object habits. In China, for example, long-standing interests in philology since the Late Qing Dynasty (1840–1912) led to enormous interest in collecting examples of hiero-glyphic texts, but as Tian (2021) has highlighted, what was valued was not the ancient inscribed objects themselves, but the traditional Chinese rubbings of them, part of the popular practice of *Jinshixue* (the study of bronze and stone).

Such collections continue to have research relevance today where originals are no longer extant and earlier translations continue to be revised, such as copies of stelae from Coptos whose translations by Wilhelm Spiegelberg have been improved by consultation with rubbings in the Peking University Museum (Clarysse and Yan 2006).

Yet the perceived value of reproductions to museums, scholarship, and education, generally waned in the mid-twentieth century following long-standing tensions between the relative importance of authentic versus representational knowledge. Many examples continue to be removed from display, such as at those at the Rijksmuseum van Oudeheden, Leiden, as part of the new gallery that opened in 2016, when 'all replicas, cases, and reconstructions had to disappear into storage in order to make room for the original artefacts' (Weiss 2018 214). The decision was predicated upon public interest. However, such removals from display do have implications for research since storage is not just a technical solution or neutral location, but a set of value judgements that have repercussions for financial investment and accessibility (Brusius and Singh 2017). Reproductions are vulnerable in store as they are rarely catalogued, leaving them open to neglect and disposal, while a lack of expertise on their material composition and documentation on how they were made has hampered conservation efforts, issues compounded by their often bulky or fragile nature.

Nevertheless, there has emerged in the twenty-first century a renewed appreciation of the value of such reproductions. Foster and Curtis (2016) have argued that replicas are archaeological things in their own right, contributing to understandings of the artefacts they are facsimiles of, providing them with a 'composite biography'. This is most obviously the case where the only surviving example is the copy, the original having been stolen or damaged (Figure 11), but also where ancient paint survives on the facsimile. Many replicas have now acquired their own patinas of age and use, inviting perceptions of 'pastness' (Holtorf 2013). They equally may embody considerable labour investment in acquisition which, like antiquities and photographs, required the apparatus of colonial structures to extract. Fortunately, collections are now subject to appraisal, as in Poland (Chudzik 2017) and Russia (Lavrentyeva 2017).

Today, there is a fresh profusion of facsimiles in museums with the advent of digital scanning and the spread of increasingly cheaper means of rendering results in a range of materials. One of the values of these physical replicas, it has been argued, lies in their representation as an 'augmented copy of the real object, on which new actions can be performed, that are otherwise not possible on the real object' (Amico et al. 2018: 118). This is the case for inaccessible artefacts, such as amulets incorporated into mummified remains (Figure 12), but it is also clearly

Figure 11 Display of Egyptian artefacts in the National Museum Jamaica in December 2019. The central item is a plaster cast of a stone statuette recovered by Egyptian teams working at Amarna for the EES's John Pendlebury in 1933. The original was sent to the Egyptian Museum Cairo, but stolen in 2011. © Alice Stevenson

evident for 'working objects' – those objects whose meanings are hard to comprehend on visual examination alone, but whose manipulation is now curtailed by museum regimes that regulate who has the skill or authority to handle them (Pye 2007). Few museum professionals today would permit the sort of

Figure 12 Image of a 3D-printed amulet (D.2016.45.1) in titanium by the
University of Liverpool Additive Manufacturing Research Team in the School
of Engineering and then hand-gilded by one of the National Museum of
Scotland's conservators for display there. The original is embedded in the
wrappings of the mummified remains of an Egyptian woman (A.1956.352)
collected by A. Henry Rhind. Image © National Museums Scotland

engagement with ancient objects like Tutankhamun's trumpet being played for
a radio broadcast in 1939, and this is where reproductions may become useful.
While 3D scanning and printing in the context of museum practice are most
commonly employed for public engagement as a means of transcending the
ocular-centric nature of display, it additionally plays a role in experimental
archaeology, which has an established history in Egyptology (Stevenson
2015a) and in the more recent emergence of sensory archaeology (Skeates and
Day 2019). In 2019, for example, Ellen Swift led a project to examine the
contribution that artefacts, including sound-making objects, make to understanding social behaviour and experience in Roman and Late Antique Egypt. Twenty
objects from the Petrie Museum were selected for replication amongst which
were bells, rattles, clappers, and panpipes (Swift et al. 2021: 289–324). Although
not manufactured using comparable technologies or materials, Swift contends
that it is still possible to examine the functional features of these objects. For
instance, this might include decibel levels and pitches, rather than the timbre of
sounds which does depend on material, thereby broadening conceptualizations of
the past beyond the visual (see Section 5.3).

In other cases, reproductions afford reconnections between museum artefacts and Egyptian landscapes. One such example comes from Spanish–Egyptian fieldwork at Dra Abu el-Naga, a hill on the West Bank near modern-day Luxor. Since 2002, the Djehuty Project team has worked around rock-cut tomb-chapels, including that of a man called Hery. This tomb, dated to *c.* 1420 BC, was plundered and heavily damaged sometime after 1896, with numerous relief-decorated wall fragments stolen and dispersed worldwide (Galán and Menéndez 2011). Prior to this, however, Wilhelm Spiegelberg had made a set of thirty-eight paper squeezes that survive today in the Griffith Institute, Oxford. These records have permitted the identification of some stolen fragments, including in the Met (50.90.4) and the Petrie Museum (UC14549). Replicas of both were sent to Egypt and incorporated into the tomb as part of its restoration and reinterpretation. In this context, the reproductions assume a greater degree of authenticity, animated within their original setting, while the museum artefact gains a composite biography more strongly tethered to that site.

While the rationale for scanning and printing the tomb relief fragments is clear, in other cases justifications for digital replication are not so evident. Rather, the technology becomes an end in itself. The appeal of digital replicas can be understood partly with reference to Gell's (1992) 'technology of enchantment' whereby art objects may be considered the result of technical processes that mystify. In this context, it is not the aesthetics of the object itself that draws wonderment, but how it has come into being. Therein lies one of the pernicious dangers of these digital technologies; they can be applied because it seems novel to do so, not because the outcomes themselves have significance. Nowhere is this more apparent than in certain applications involving mummified remains. In 2020, the prestigious journal *Nature Scientific Reports* published a study involving a 3D-printed vocal tract from the body of Nesyamun (1106–1107 BC) and whose mummified remains are in Leeds City Museum (Howard et al. 2020). A vowel sound was produced by blowing through the reproduction, which the study's authors claimed allowed 'people to engage with the past in completely new and innovative ways'. The paper was sensationally reported in the World's media, but its epistemological value was limited. Criticism was widespread (Matić 2020), highlighting the superficial justifications for the research that 'Nesyamun's own words express his desire to "speak again"', itself a misunderstanding of ancient Egyptian beliefs and sidestepping more serious ethical concerns (Riggs 2014). Far from providing any insight into the ancient past, this appropriation underscores more recent fetishization with the perceived abilities of science to further understanding.

The popular move towards 3D prints, while expedient, also leads to further questions. Why, for instance, are other more traditional replication tools, in comparable materials not more suitable research methods since they may help give insight into a wider range of haptic senses and skills involved in an object's creation than 3D production does? Such senses include texture and weight, which leads investigators to negotiate their reproductions directly with original objects to ascertain production processes, whereas a 3D print reproduces an object at a specific point its biography privileging its visual rather than material qualities (Cooper 2019). Zinn's (2018) investigation of unprovenanced ancient Egyptian headrests in Cyfarthfa Castle Museum and Art Gallery employing reproductions in different types of wood is one example that highlights the value of engaging with a range of materials.

Like all collections, modern replicas are implicated within the politics of acquisition that raise serious concerns, such their ownership, application, and reception. Digital media is not a neutral tool. It is entangled with communication norms, embedded logics, and complex permissions. While it is tempting, for instance, to refer to the integration of museum replicas into original sites, like the Dra Abu el-Naga reliefs, as a form of digital repatriation, to do so undermines the efficacy of repatriation and what it stands for (Boast and Enote 2013). Moreover, while the physical copy may have been sent to Egypt, the digital data associated with the scan of the original were not, issues that compound the digital divide. The contentious issue of ownership was highlighted by artists Nora Al-Badri and Jan Nikolai Nelles with their creation, *The Other Nefertiti*. It involved a 3D print of the bust of Nefertiti held by the Neues Museum, Berlin, together with its associated digital data which were released into the public domain in 2015 (Elias 2019; Geismar 2018). While the artists claimed that the data had been procured through clandestine scanning of the bust in the gallery (public photography of the bust is strictly prohibited), investigative journalism suggested that the source was a high-resolution scan commissioned by the Neues Museum itself. As that data had not been publicly accessible previously it is presumed to have been hacked. Regardless of the truth, the incident underscores how museums retain control over not just cultural goods, but digital assets and it draws attention to the 'interface between different material forms, and between objects and people' (Geismar 2018: 112).

These are pressing issues given the exponential increase of born-digital data across the field sciences and humanities, and the rise of the 'post-digital museum'. The latter term reflects how the digital is becoming normative within all areas of museum practice, blurring the distinction between 'digital' and 'non-digital' (Parry 2013). This is clear from museum approaches that identify digital materials as objects in their own right, such as images of African rock art in the British Museum which have been collected digitally and formally accessioned into the collection. The project entailed working through issues similar to those of artefact curation; issues of preservation, storage, documentation, research, and access (Anderson et al. 2018). Just as those who are researching museum collections of photographs undertake a forensic material analysis through being attuned to the traces, inscriptions, and residues of past engagements with such assemblages, so too will future scholars approaching digital objects. A museum sensibility is therefore vital to understand for researchers heading out into the field in Egypt, so as to give them perspective on how their recording techniques, which increasingly will move towards digital methods, may stand up to historical scrutiny.

3.3 Restoration and Conservation

Between original and reproduction lies practices that add modern materials in order to stabilize, preserve, or restore artefacts. In the case of material from Egypt there is a well-documented history of techniques and approaches to the treatment of antiquities, both shortly after excavation in the field (Odegaard and O'Grady 2016) and in the museum (Gänsicke et al. 2003). Some interventions were driven by expectations that objects should appear fully intact and visually harmonious. Several proved to be physically deleterious over time for the objects or have contaminated them to such a degree that archaeological research into their properties or age is inhibited with analysis picking up on more recent conservation efforts rather than ancient signatures. For instance, adhesives and consolidants (e.g. Paraloid B72) may disrupt radiocarbon dating (Fedi et al. 2014). More insidious, Stable et al. (2021) suggest, was the role of restoration 'in repurposing objects' for foreign institutions, justifying their export to places that had the expertise to care for them. At the National Museum of Scotland these trends in the 1950s to 1970s under Egyptologist Cyril Aldred, who presented an art historical rather than archaeological approach to display, led to extensive intercessions. These aimed to convey to the public 'a perfected vision of Ancient Egypt' (Stable et al. 2021: 148), blurring repair and restoration, alterations that have been normalized through long-term display and widespread publication. Returning these constructs nearer to the form in which artefacts were found or otherwise extracted from Egypt is a negotiation of factors such as ensuring structural integrity, establishing treatment stability, evaluating interpretive possibilities, and assessing the historical significance of the conservation intervention itself. Moreover, what constitutes an original state or an object's 'authentic self', can be highly contentious and it may be desirable to preserve indications of the passage of time. Conservation, like any museum practice, emerges not as a neutral technical procedure but as an interpretive act (Sweetnam and Henderson 2022).

A ripple-flaked knife in the Pitt Rivers Museum, Oxford, provides an example (Figure 13). At some point in the last century a conservator painstakingly realigned the fragments of this 5500-year-old lithic so that it was immaculate for display. Few pieces of flintwork of any age, from any country come close to the technical mastery that such prehistoric artefacts embody. However, this knife was not made to be preserved and displayed, but to be broken and buried. It was found in several pieces during the 1911 excavations of a cemetery near the modern village of Gerzeh, concealed for millennia under a heavy pile of gravel (Stevenson 2009: 113). Although seemingly delicate, its fragmentation was not accidental; many such knives reveal the same, distinctive pattern of breakage radiating outwards from their centres. These were acts of deliberate destruction, achieved with a short, sharp punch, probably part of the funeral performance itself. As 'objects of enchantment' (Gell 1992) these were potent things that consumed and radiated effort and emotion. In the unwitting attempt to mute the ancient drama that those jagged shards materialize, its repair might be viewed as another kind of destruction. For what was concealed here was not the accidental ravages of time, but the purposeful intentions of a brief and intense moment in the past, now silenced.

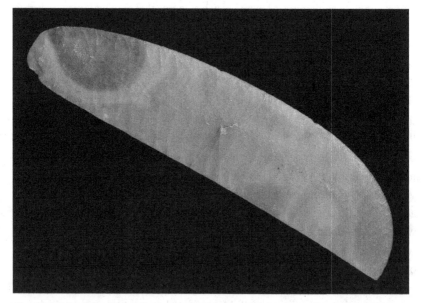

Figure 13 Fourth millennium BC ripple flaked knife from Gerzeh, Egypt, Pitt Rivers Museum after conservation (1911.33.1). Courtesy of the Pitt Rivers Museum

For archaeologists, context has long been deemed integral to interpretation. Too often that context has been used to simply authenticate or to date an object that is otherwise deemed to have inherent value and meaning. But context provides much more than a classificatory reference point; it offers a set of parameters for inferring how an artefact was made meaningful. There is an important distinction here, one that emphasizes the traces of practice and process rather than product. Frequently, it is such traces that have historically been erased to facilitate collection and display. Riggs (2014) has highlighted this issue with regard to the swathes of linen wrappings that enveloped statues and religious objects in the tomb of Tutankhamun (Figure 14). These were discarded by the excavators and, as a result, their significance was overlooked by Egyptologists. The excavators, Riggs surmises, likely viewed the linen swaddling as mere storage solutions, equivalent to the buffers that aided the transport and storage of artefacts for museums. Her detailed study makes it clear though that these wrappings were as important as what was wrapped, since this both bestowed and signalled the sacred (Riggs 2014: 23). Similarly, sticky

Figure 14 Linen-wrapped statuettes of Geb (Carter no. 299), Sakhmet (no. 300), Kebehsenuf and Duamutef (no. 304) from Tutankhamun's tomb. Burton photograph 1665 © Griffith Institute, University of Oxford

aromatic resin-oils poured over some objects in the tomb as an integral part of their ritual anointment were painstakingly removed by Carter's team turning them 'into artworks fit for a museum vitrine' (Riggs 2021: 27). This was a common practice throughout the twentieth century, with residues on anthropoid coffins and cartonnage cases from the early first millennium BC also removed during conservation to reveal the underlying decoration (Moser and Nicola 2017).

In these instances, not only have the traces of ancient practices been rendered invisible but so too have many of the modern interventions so crucial to the creation of their modern identities as 'artworks'. Conservators have more recently sought means to make their work distinguishable from past materials and re-treatable, but those interventions usually remain discrete. A 'disruptive conservation', on the other hand, is a provocation for conservators to consider how their remediations might be made more dramatically visible, underscoring the role that they play in the life of an object and highlighting the fact that all objects are always in the process of becoming (Sweetnam and Henderson 2022). In such a fashion, multi-directionality might be materialized with different histories of practice colliding and coexisting.

4 Space and Place

On 3 April 2021, the mummified bodies of twenty-two ancient Egyptian royals were spectacularly paraded through the empty streets of an otherwise unusually quiet Cairo. Under a strict curfew from the Egyptian state, a route had been secured for armoured security vehicles, dressed to resemble chariots, to transport the remains from the Egyptian Museum in Tahrir Square to the newly built National Museum of Egyptian Civilization (NMEC) in Fustat (Figure 15), where Egypt's modern-day ruler, President Sisi, presided over their arrival. As noted by Carruthers (2021): 'Moving south from Tahrir Square to the city founded under ʿAmr ibn al-ʿAs in AD 641 (itself located in close proximity to the Roman fortress of Babylon and the compound of 'Coptic Cairo'), the procession neatly tied together the periods of Egyptian history connected to the state's telling of its past'.

Time has long had a spatial configuration in Egypt's museum landscape. Across the urban fabric of Cairo and Alexandria separate institutions demarcate pharaonic Egypt, Greco-Roman Egypt, Coptic, and Islamic pasts (Doyon 2008). Recent developments have begun to physically disrupt the location of these periods with new museum buildings like the UNESCO-backed NMEC, but also the internationally financed 3,800-acre Grand Egyptian Museum (GEM) in Cairo, together with a host of state-of-the-art regional museums

Figure 15 Photograph of the National Museum of Egyptian Civilization, Fustat, in February 2017. © Alice Stevenson

across the country. Notably, some are presenting a wider spectrum of cultural heritage than has generally been the case for galleries of 'ancient Egypt' outside of the country. The protracted negotiations over which collections were to be housed in which of these institutions were not merely technical; they manifest new localities of professional and cultural identities that have implications for intellectual demarcations and research priorities, with new laboratories and conservation spaces accompanying the vast exhibition halls and storage units. What are the consequences for the future shape of Egyptology in Egypt as a result?

The burgeoning museum sector in Egypt throws into relief the power of new, iconic museum structures and the possibilities for alternative juxtapositions and framing. All have the potential to challenge disciplinary canons and to materialize conceptual geographies that unsettle presentations of a monolithic Egypt. Equally, however, they reveal the continuation of traditional modes of presentation, the neocolonial bases of globalized museum productions, and the politics of representation. This section draws from the spatial turn in the analysis of knowledge production, which has emphasized the constitutive significance of place in the establishment of theories and practice (Livingstone 2003). Beginning with the buildings themselves, the below examines how museum architecture temporally frames Egyptian representations within them, as well the locations of those buildings, before considering more conceptual geographies, such as the position of Egypt vis-à-vis other regions of the world, including the continent of Africa.

4.1 Buildings

Architecture is not simply a platform or backdrop for representation or interpretation, but an experiential environment that shapes the conditions of seeing, experiencing, and knowing. Scholars, such as Duncan (1995), have demonstrated the ways in which museums are not neutral, transparent sheltering spaces as might frequently be assumed, likening them instead to ceremonial monuments in which museumgoers shift into a certain state of receptivity. Hurley (2020), for example, has examined the staging of Egypt in nineteenth-century European museums and how they sought to affectively frame their collections. Some situated their collections within well-established neoclassical decorative schemes, as in the Louvre or British Museum. Played out on the walls of those museums were tensions between different intellectual discourses on Egypt's place in the history of cultures, particularly between the intersection of Greece and Egypt (Moser 2006). In other institutions more elaborate rooms, embellished with richly decorated and coloured scenes copied from Egyptian tombs, surrounded Egyptian antiquities, like those in Berlin's Neues Museum that opened in 1850, based on designs by Prussian Egyptologist Karl Lepsius. Further examples include the Kunsthistorisches Museum which opened in Vienna in 1891 and the National Archaeological Museum in Naples (Figure 16). These vignettes created an immersive environment that sought to enliven what were sometimes rather humble objects (Bodenstein 2012). Although painted to afford visitors an insight into the significance of individual objects, in reality these frescos imparted an overarching history and philosophy of knowledge, emphasizing the installation as whole over the artefacts per se. The effect of the Valley of the Kings inspired murals in Naples was further enhanced by the sloping curves of the museum's vaulted basement in which the

Figure 16 Paolo Vetri's painting *Museo* 1875, held in the Palazzo Zevallos
Stigliano, Naples, showing the late nineteenth-century mural painting used to
frame Egyptian antiquities in the Archaeological Museum in Naples.
Photographed by Silko from https://commons.wikimedia.org/wiki/File:
Paolo_vetri,_museo,_1875,_01.JPG#globalusage
Creative Commons Attribution 3.0.

galleries were situated, a location that was disastrous for the preservation of the
objects due to the damp conditions, but whose architecture was deemed apropos
since it evoked tomb-like structures, albeit Eurocentric in impression. For
decades these surrounds lent the galleries 'a macabre and funerary view of
Egyptian civilization' (Borriello and Giove 2000: 12).

One surviving set of mural paintings is in the Neues Museum, rendered onto
what was originally the 'Egyptian hall' and featuring images of Egyptian
landscapes and monuments. These were largely covered up or else destroyed
in World War II but were resurrected in architect David Chipperfield's salvage
renovation that opened in 2009. His project was not an explicit restoration of
these images, but instead a self-historicization, placing murals from the 1850s
and 1860s into twenty-first century museum narratives. In so doing, the
museum's own historical role in forging perceptions of the past was brought
to the fore. As Bodenstein observes, the museum through these means creates
a double temporality: 'By becoming "historical," it breaks with the perception
of the museum space as an atemporal and neutral backdrop for the presentation
of historicized objects' (Bodenstein 2012: 270).

Chipperfield's careful adaptation of ruins cast the surrounds themselves as exhibit, a strategy that has been largely celebrated. However, a recurrent theme in discussions concerning contemporary museum design are the tensions created by spectacular, iconic buildings designed by so-called 'star-architects', which are often criticized as indulgences dislocated from their contents and messages (MacLeod 2005: 2). There are cases where the design of space has sought to speak to the collections they contain, such as the Staatliches Museum Ägyptischer Kunst, Munich, which was relocated to a new subterranean space that opened in June 2013. It was designed by architect Peter Böhm and inspired by ancient Egyptian burial chambers, with an entrance area created to evoke the pylon gateways of New Kingdom temples. While this represents an architectural effort to speak inwardly to the collection, rather than to project a signature landmark outwards, the modern materials of concrete, the minimalist exhibitionary design, and the limited interpretive supports are more redolent of the modern art gallery where the modus operandi is to ensure that nothing distracts from the art on display. Each individual sculpture is given ample space in individual vitrines with the aim of inviting concentrated contemplation. They are positioned under spotlights so that they seem to radiate off their own volition, endowing them with an air of mystery seeming to appear beyond time. But it is a display strategy which parallels well-established contemporary art gallery aesthetics, assimilating these objects within twentieth-century viewing cultures, subjecting artefacts from different cultures and periods to Western conceptions of 'art' (Barker 1999).

Such viewing conditions do shape interpretive focus and value judgements. When objects are not treated to conditions that generate museal aura, their serious assessment can be neglected. An example is the inscription of Weni the Elder, subject of a revealing analysis by Richards (2002). The text is considered one of the principle 'autobiographical' accounts of the late third millennium BC, detailing Weni's service as Governor of Upper Egypt under three pharaohs. The stela on which this text was inscribed was excavated at Abydos in 1860 from where it was transported to Cairo. While the historical account rose to prominence, becoming one of the standard texts of study for students of Egyptology, little attention was given to the artefact on which the autobiography was originally carved. Richards notes famed Egyptologist Gardiner's disdain of the object itself, which he considered to be 'an insignificant looking slab of stone', a perception shaped by its museum setting in a poorly lit and densely populated corner of the Egyptian Museum. Closer examination by Richards, however, revealed the monumentality of the stela and the quality of the text's execution, which is of increased significance when contextualized within the landscape in which it was once erected.

Removing objects from their traditional museum sanctums, whether in storage or on display, into other locations for engagement with communities that might not visit museums can also provide insights into the material properties and histories of things. These activities are most usually undertaken as educational outreach exercises by institutions, such as in the form of school loan boxes. More recently this concept has extended to other sites of encounter under the aegis of health and well-being initiatives. Staff at the Museo Egizo in Turin, for instance, devised projects that have taken replica museum collections into places such as hospitals and prisons (Del Vesco 2022). A different approach is the model of the 'pop-up' museum in which museum objects, displays, and events are accommodated into existing sites of contemporary life such as shops, libraries, cafes, pubs, or stations, allowing people to encounter museum objects unexpectedly. The Fitzwilliam Museum's 'Egypt Coffins Project' held a series of 'pop-up' events in both the United Kingdom and Cairo in 2019, with the explicit objective of taking research beyond the museum's wall to new audiences. One location, however, was especially productive in terms of developing fresh research itself; the furniture production centre of Damietta, Egypt, leading to encounters with modern craft-workers who brought new ways of thinking and alternative questions regarding ancient Egyptian coffin manufacture (Pitkin 2019).

4.2 Egypt in Egypt

In Egypt, the Egyptian Museum in Cairo on Tahrir Square has, since 1901, been the primary site for the consumption of the country's antiquities. The building was designed within the Parisian Beaux Arts tradition by French architect Marcel-Lazare Dourgnon. With its arches, domes, columns, and halls surrounding the sky-lit court it was a manifestation of Europe's appropriation of the pharaonic past (Reid 2002: 195). In contrast, Heneghan Peng's design (chosen after an international competition) for the GEM takes its cue from the Giza plateau where it is situated, forming a new edge to the existing landscape, 'architecturalizing' it, and orientating it with a view towards Cairo and the pyramids (Heneghan Peng Architects n.d.). Yet this location on the edge of Cairo outside of the contemporary urban expanse and its civic centres – in part a legacy of Mubarak-era priorities to create new secure, elite, gated developments rather than enhance old historic infrastructures – has been seen as exclusionary, alienating the majority of Egyptians from accessing it (Elshahed 2015). In a country with a 29.7 per cent poverty rate, the investment and state pageantry that accompanies GEM's profile, speaks volumes about the centrality of the past to the contemporary government's agenda (Elnozahy 2021) and to the tourism so central to the country's economy (El Nagar and Derbali 2020). GEM largely restricts its chronological range to Egyptology's traditional colonial purview between prehistory and the end of the Roman era. As Elshahed (2015) observed, the decision to relocate Tutankhamun's tomb assemblage here, in view of the pyramids, further ensures the alignment of touristic expectations of Egypt, equating the 'Grand' of 'Egyptian' with the ancient past. Such curatorial resolutions, Levitt and Parrs (2019) contend, have also to be understood within a broader museum ecology, a network of museums that implicitly or explicitly work in tandem, with changes in one influencing the direction of another. Thus, while GEM projects a national narrative, institutions such as the Coptic Museum are left to convey more detailed histories that are not centrally included in the national narratives or in the global hierarchy of cultural institutions (Levitt and Parrs 2019).

Beyond the centres of Cairo, Alexandria, and Luxor, Egyptological material has historically been more widely spread and more accessible outside of, rather than within Egypt itself. Following the 1952 establishment of the Republic, some palaces were transformed into museums, but it was not until the mid-1970s that regional museums emerged across the country in any number (Doyon 2008). Nevertheless, such institutions were not constructed with local inhabitants in mind, but for foreign tourists, assets facilitating economic development rather than cultural spaces that accommodated Egyptian needs (Rashed 2015). In the twenty-first century, the museum landscape has begun to change with new museums that bridge the gap between ancient and modern Egypt (Eissa and el-Senussi 2020). As of 2021, there are around fifty museums in Egypt devoted to historical themes, many of which have expanded beyond Egyptology's divisions to convey a richer spectrum of cultural traditions and artistic expressions (Rashed 2015). NMEC's mission, for instance, is to represent the full range of Egyptian history from prehistory to the present day, encompassing tangible and intangible heritage (el-Moniem 2005). It is a strategy being increasingly adopted throughout Egypt as new regional museums are established. The Sharm el-Sheikh Museum in Egypt's Sinai Peninsula, for example, was opened in October 2020 with collections not just from pharaonic Egypt and Greco-Roman Egypt, but also material representing Islamic and Bedouin heritage (Hassanein and Kamal 2021).

This recent enterprise of intensive museum construction is a continuation of Egyptian museums' and collections' role in the exercise of soft power, bound up with the State's interests in a nationalist projection of global modernity. The ongoing musealization of Egypt is most starkly evident in the development of museum displays within the country's airports, bringing together two significant poles of late-industrial and post-industrial urbanism. Airports are non-places in many regards, a 'consumerist hyper-void' (Pellizzi 2008: 338) in which the museum tries to create a sense of local colour. The Cairo International Airport Museum (Terminal 3) was inaugurated in 2016, followed in May 2021 by a further set of displays of some 300 artefacts in Terminal 2. Together the museums cover the Predynastic through to Coptic and Islamic cultures and are the first of several planned displays in airports across Egypt. The artefacts might be unable to legally transit out of the country, but they nevertheless project a clear message of continuity between the ancient past and contemporary present not just in the juxtapositions of objects from a wide chronological range, but also by their setting.

Much of Egyptian heritage, both in Egypt and in institutions abroad, is not on display however, but held in storage (Eissa and el-Senussi 2020). Fieldwork has often been framed in terms of a 'crisis narrative' whereby the archaeological record needs protection, rescue, or preservation lest it be lost. Yet in museums there have been decades of panic over a very different crisis; the 'curation crisis' in which there is simply too much archaeology and it is an issue worldwide (Kersel 2015). It is a particularly acute problem within Egypt itself given the density, frequency, and profile of archaeological excavations. Display strategies may put singular pieces onto a pedestal, but behind the scenes the mainstay of archaeological collections is 'bulk finds'[5] numbering in the hundreds of thousands with enormous research potential, but difficult to access. In Egypt, most are retained in storage magazines at archaeological sites, where suitable environmental conditions, documentation, and security are often insufficient, limiting opportunities for research and engagement (Elnaggar 2014). Like many parts of the world, Europe and North America included, the overemphasis upon new fieldwork without due consideration and budgeting for the products of those projects has led to an unsustainable situation. Better archaeological training that integrates collections and a museum sensibility might be one means of addressing these oversights so that post-excavation needs are accounted for at the outset of field projects.

4.3 Egypt in Africa

In 1973, the Brooklyn Museum staged a two-month exhibition, *Akhenaten and Nefertiti. Art from the Age of the Sun King* features 170 examples of 'Amarna art' (Figure 17). The museum, situated within a borough that is home to a substantial population of African Americans (at the time estimated to be

---

[5] While museums may individually number artefacts, often it is not practicable to individually number and catalogue all archaeological finds. Bulk accessioning is thus adopted, whereby one accession number covers multiple objects.

Figure 17 An example of Amarna art. Black and white photography of a relief carving showing Akhenaten and Nefertiti found during the Egypt Explorations Society's 1926–1927 excavations at Amarna. Courtesy of the Egypt Exploration Society (TA.NEG.26-27-073)

a quarter of the demographic of Brooklyn), just five years previously had opened a community gallery in response to demands made by local Black artists for their work to be showcased. This proactive Black community was especially drawn to the central characters of the new Egyptian show, both of whom had become icons of Afrocentrist history (Montserrat 2000: 116–23). Yet many were offended by what they read on the labels. They were also offended by what they did not read; that Egypt was in Africa and that Egyptians were Black. Their dismay was recorded in a publication devoted to the visitor comments (Wedge 1977: 53–9). A curatorial response by Bothmer was included, in which he expressed surprise at seeing statements 'again and again that Egypt was part of ancient Africa – which shows how many people saw this an exhibition of African rather than Near Eastern art' (Wedge 1977: 157). His comment highlights the curatorial assumptions that underpinned the collection's presentation which privileged a Eurocentric geography – the Near East – itself burdened with specific value-laden categories of cultural difference. One such term that riled many African American visitors was the word 'grotesque', used negatively as a description for Akhenaten's image:

Akneten [*sic*] grotesque, he was a beautiful black man.
When one speaks of deformities it should not imply that negroid features are
unnaturally developed. Your exhibit is racist.

'Grotesque' is a term with a complex usage in art history, but one tied to
White, European canons of beauty. It is not a neutral descriptor for the
deviation from previous representations of Egyptian kingship that Amarna
art constitutes.

Bothmer tellingly referred to some of the views expressed as 'militant',
presuming by default a benign Egyptological scholarship, an assumption also
reflected in his claim that 'an art exhibition is the last place to discourse on
ethnic questions' (Wedge 1977: 157–8). The history of the discipline demonstrates otherwise, with the vehement, but erroneous denunciation of ancient
Egypt's African origins strenuously made by Petrie, Reisner, and their colleagues driven by racialized biases that justified their contemporary societal
constructs (Minor 2018). There is a strong genealogy of Black intellectual
rebuttal of these spurious claims, including by Du Bois (Davies 2019–20), but
it is only more recently that work from within Egyptology and Classics is
highlighting the nature and implications of these histories (Challis 2013;
Johnson 2021; Matić 2020). These latter works do not argue that modern
inventions of 'race' should be applied to ancient objects anachronistically, but
rather that they raise awareness of representational schemas that have contributed to constructions of race in the first place. More concerningly, these
assumptions continue to underpin contemporary archaeological interpretations
(Matić 2020). These works offer a vital critical disruption to historical imagin-
ations of the past, what in our mind's eye we reach for when we consciously or
unconsciously visualize the people behind the material culture in museum
repositories, whether ancient or more recent.

A multi-directional curation in the twenty-first century, therefore, needs to be
cognisant of how words, interpretations, and representations cross-reference
and resonate beyond disciplines, refracting the present on the past and vice
versa. The position of mummified human remains within museums is a case in
point. The *Illustrated London News (ILN)* reported on 13 February 1847 that the
British Museum's Mummy room 'has usually crowds of visitors'. More than
a century later the background noise in the first radio broadcast episode of the
British Museum's *History of the World* is the hubbub of people; 'It's a pretty
safe bet' MacGregor comments 'that most of the children you can hear round
about me are also headed for the Egyptian mummies'. Viewing the mummified
Egyptian dead in museums has become a Western cultural tradition (Day 2016:
32). But what if we began with a different history of encounter? Trafton (2004:

222–3) recounts an early nineteenth-century visit made by a free African American to Baltimore's Rembrandt Peale Museum, which housed one of the first pharaonic remains to be displayed in the USA. In 1827, he reported in the abolitionist weekly *Freedom's Journal* that 'as a descendant of Cush I could not but mourn her present degradation'. He went on to ask, 'Have they not been torn from the "vaulted sepulchres," and exhibited to a gazing world? Have not they too been bought and sold?' From early on it is clear that the encounter with Egyptian human remains was for many African Americans a reminder of slavery, of bodies abused for White gain. In the following century Du Bois (1947: 99) would note that '[I]t is especially significant that the science of Egyptology arose and flourished at the very time that the cotton kingdom reached its greatest power on the foundation of American Negro slavery'. More recently, Saini's (2019) *Superior: The Return of Race Science* opens in the British Museum reflecting on the Egyptian remains, a mausoleum she remarks, in which racial categories have, and continue to be, given meaning. Here, distinct histories confront and inform each other, as Rothberg (2009) contended. Furthermore, it highlights that not only do museums need to consider source communities, but also 'communities of implication' – those who may be affected by tangible or intangible cultural products in ethical terms (Lehrer 2020: 304). This does not undermine fundamental legal or ethical imperatives in the recognition of 'source communities', including Egyptians (Abd el-Gawad and Stevenson in press) for whom relationships with such positionalities are complex (see Aïdi 2022), but it does allow institutions to expand notions of object–community relations and the range of voices that museums bring to bear on their holdings.

An African Egypt is becoming better developed in US museums (Cummins 2016), but museums elsewhere have acknowledged the African context of Egypt, such as the Fitzwilliam Museum in Cambridge (Ashton 2011). They are generally temporary exhibitions. Reconfiguring permanent displays occurs far less often. One experiment was conducted at the Horniman Museum in London, when the African Worlds gallery was opened in 1999 and maintained until 2016 (Stevenson and Williams in press). It was the United Kingdom's first permanent African exhibition with a focus on past and present relationships between Africa and Europe, highlighting the contribution of African cultures to common world heritage (Shelton 2000). One of the strategies adopted was a rebranding of Egypt as *Kemet*, a term that has become synonymous with the Afrocentric and Black Power movement for the intellectual repatriation of ancient Egyptian heritage from the West (Asante 1995). This revisionist 'whole Africa' approach signified an attempt to combat the colonial image of Africa defined by a 'Sub-Saharan' traditional, tribal existence (Phillips 2002). However, the restriction of Egypt's identity to a purely ancient culture undermined this. Despite considerable periods of relevant ethnographic collecting by the Museum, the selection of objects for display excluded contemporary Egyptian and North African material, reinforcing an image prevalent in museum histories; that of an Africa without Arabic-speaking countries. The further exclusion of Egyptian material culture from community engagement during the gallery's construction reinforced the idea that the study and cultural 'ownership' of ancient Egypt is the privilege of Western specialist knowledge (Ashton 2011). With the African Gallery's refurbishment in 2018, a World Cultures gallery took its place, arranged by continent and developed through co-curation with source communities, recognizing their ongoing relationships with heritage. Egypt's place was eroded once more, with the popular displays of ancient Egyptian funerary items reinstalled in the balcony overlooking the main gallery below and not subject to the same co-curation ethos of the primary displays.

The Horniman Museum's African Worlds gallery highlights the vexed position of Egyptian material culture in relation to other regions of the world and assumptions regarding the isolation of Egyptian cultures (Schneider 2007). The place of Nubia and Sudan, the Mediterranean, Western Asia, and other interconnections are often peripheral rather than integral to understanding Egyptian material, identities, and histories. Egypt's seclusion in museum displays has had a large role to play in codifying this particular canon of exceptional, independent 'Egyptian art' and its chronotopic features. The scholarship in this vein is 'shaped around the conventions of museology' and has hindered, Kreiter (2020) argues, wider understandings of ancient Egypt, while overshadowing the agency and significance of the peoples and cultures of surrounding regions. Take, for instance, the contrast in the Met, where Islamic Egyptian material is presented in discrete galleries devoted to Islamic or Asian culture rather than Egyptian, although such a separation is not similarly recognized for Nubian material (Fazzini 1995). One of the largest collections of Nubian and Sudanese material in North America is held by the Boston Museum of Fine Arts, from fieldwork led by George Reisner in the early twentieth century. Little of this was ever published and historically the museum rarely displayed much of this vast collection. A dedicated gallery existed between 1991 and 2006, and a special exhibition, *Ancient Nubia Now,* was showcased in 2020 (Figure 18), acknowledging the racist history of interpretation and including the voices of Sudanese diaspora communities (Emberling 2020). The show is one of an increasing number of exhibitions devoted to the subject of Nubia and Sudan in the twenty-first century, in part reflecting contemporary geopolitics whereby Egyptologists, finding it more difficult to secure fieldwork in Egypt, have shifted focus to a seemingly more accessible field. Yet, as Sudan faces ongoing civil unrest

Figure 18 Photograph of a text panel used in the 2020 *Ancient Nubia Now* exhibition at the Museum of Fine Arts, Boston. © Amanda Ford Spora

efforts may well turn towards the collections previously secured, where there is a moral obligation to publish and make it broadly accessible.

5 Experimental Reassembling

The British Museum should not be looked on as a collection of dead art discon-nected from our own times. (Moore, cited in Putnam and Davies 1994: 59)

As a young sculptor, Henry Moore (1898–1986) drew inspiration from museum galleries, spending hours amongst Egyptian statuary. As an elderly and world-famous artist, he acknowledged that debt in a generous donation to the British Museum's Egyptian Sculpture Gallery renovation, completed in 1981. The list of prominent, twentieth-century artists influenced by ancient Egyptian material culture is extensive including Pablo Picasso, Barbara Hepworth, Alberto Giacometti, and Mahmoud Mukhtar. Their works rarely occupy the same institutional spaces as their ancient muses, most being exhibited in contemporary art galleries or other public spaces. From the 1990s onwards, temporary juxtapositions of ancient and modern art became more commonplace, usually to highlight the unidirectional influence of ancient upon modern times. But might the reverse be true? What new insights into or theories about ancient Egypt might these re-combinations lead to? Or, are they merely another form of aestheticization and modern appropriation? Can the trend of employing contemporary artists become part of knowledge production in Egyptology? This section argues that it can.

There is an emergent literature on exhibition experiments which highlights how exhibitionary practice – through marshalling curators, artefacts, technologies, visitors, and architectural space – is experimental, providing a site for the generation, rather than the reproduction, of ideas and experience (Deliss 2012; MacDonald and Basu 2007). It is here that there is an opportunity to mix media and to juxtapose Egyptology collections within alternative disciplinary traditions, telescope temporalities, and move towards a multi-directional mode of discourse. Most striking within this vein of practice are the interventions from artists seeking to disrupt dominant modes of interpretation, but contemporary collecting of a wider range of materials than just antiquities equally offers fresh opportunities for disciplinary development. While previous sections have looked at histories, materials, and sites, this section looks towards how these might be reconfigured in a multi-directional framework, including the assembly of new materials and histories through contemporary collecting.

5.1 Contemporary Art

In 2014, if you were to enter the first gallery of Egyptian art at the Staatliches Museum Ägyptischer Kunst, Munich, it would not have been the ancient art that first caught your eye, but a luminous neon installation by Maurizio Nannucci proclaiming that 'ALL ART HAS BEEN CONTEMPORARY' (Figure 19), part of the wider *Nofretet téte-a-téte* exhibition curated by art duo Sam Bardaouil and Till Fellrath. While material from Egypt's past has long inspired contemporary artists, the genre of artistic interventions instead involves placing

Figure 19 Installation by Maurizio Nannucci 'ALL ART HAS BEEN CONTEMPORARY' part of *Nofretet – téte-a-téte* exhibition curated by art duo Sam Bardaouil and Till Fellrath at the Staatliches Museum Ägyptischer Kunst in Munich, 2014. © Alice Williams

modern interlocutors within pre-existing displays. Here, artists might not just take inspiration from collections but also juxtapose them with historical exhibits in order to disrupt authoritative representations (La 2011).

Since the 1990s, contemporary artistic interventions and 'artist in residence' programmes have become a popular means of bringing novel perspectives to displays, including those devoted to ancient Egypt. Early features include *Time Machine–Ancient Egypt and Contemporary Art* curated by James Putnam at the British Museum between December 1994 and February 1995. The exhibition brought together twelve newly commissioned works constituting the first large-scale artistic intervention at a major UK museum. It reportedly brought in new audiences (Roberts 2013: 13), a key motivator for invigorating display strategies. But what would these new visitors take away from the encounter? Could such interventions change how Egyptologists think about the collections or how they interpreted the past? Historical precedence suggests it might. Montserrat (2000) demonstrated how the language of the art nouveau movement permeated Petrie's effusive 1892 descriptions of the Great Palace at Amarna (c.1350 BC); the 'naturalistic grace of the plants' and 'the new style of art'. In other words, the art of Petrie's day helped him to describe an unfamiliar past and to interpret unusual finds. The resonance between ancient and modern times, Montserrat argued, was not simply a casual or convenient point of reference but interpretive, implying a comparable ideology that rejected designs predicated upon renaissance or classical forms. Moser (2019) suggests that a similar relationship existed between artists and archaeologists in her investigation of nineteenth-century artists Alma-Tadema, Poynter, and Long, in the creation of perspectives on ancient Egypt.

One of the challenges seen to adopting contemporary works as interpretive frameworks is that they are explicitly subjective. Indeed, they are frequently left uninterpreted, meaning that the extent to which they help, or hinder, interpretations has been questioned. Merriman (2004), for example, has queried the use of artists as they overly emphasize the aesthetic at the expense of contextualization and interpretation. He has suggested instead 'informed imagination',

> ... an approach to interpretation which is based on the knowledge of the archaeological and historical context of the material provided by the expertise of the curators, but which acknowledges diversity of views, the contingency of archaeological interpretations, and encourages imagination and enjoyment in the visitors' own constructions of the past. (Merriman 2004: 102)

A lack of contextualization can be raised for *Time Machine*, since although such interventions might demonstrate the impact of Egyptian art on contemporary artists, their works rarely speak back to the original objects. These are simply 'insertions' rather than interventions (La 2011: 232). Thus, while the theme of the exhibition was bridging past and present, arguably what was achieved was a state of timelessness, an extension of the museum's usual practice. A similar observation has been made of contemporary art projects in Egypt, many staged by a private firm called Art D'Égypte. The initiative was responsible for a 2017 exhibition at the Egyptian Museum, *Eternal Light: Something Old, Something New*, which set sixteen contemporary artworks from Egyptian artists beside antiquities inside the museum. Like *Time Machine*, it has been argued that the artworks lacked depth and relevance, functioning only as devices of static contemporaneity to imbue the space with further cultural significance according to institutional norms and nationalistic agendas (Elnozahy 2021).

Nevertheless, art interventions can challenge the very expertise of curators and archaeologists by interrogating and destabilizing foundational interpretive frameworks. Institutional critique, for instance, strives to expose the workings of museums and bring about transformation in relations of power (Alberro 2009: 3). The African American conceptual artist Fred Wilson is strongly associated with institutional critique and has long-standing interests in ancient

Egypt and its museum representation. His best-known work, *Grey Area*, takes the bust of Nefertiti in the Neues Museum, Berlin, as its subject and was originally part of the installation *Re:Claiming Egypt* for the 1992 Cairo Biennale. It comprises five identical copies of the bust, each in a different shade from black through greys to white. In so doing, Wilson brought attention to the Eurocentrism of Egyptological representations and racial assumptions regarding Egyptian skin colour (Riggs 2017a: 159–60). The piece was later acquired by the Tate Modern, London, where its critical specificity is unfortunately muted by its physical separation from the institutions that hold Egyptian antiquities. A second iteration, *Grey Area (Brown Version)* was acquired by Brooklyn Museum of Fine Arts, which does hold Egyptian collections. The artwork, however, is displayed in a separate gallery.

Wilson has additionally explored stored museum collections through his 1997 *In the Course of Arrangement* installed into British Museum's Egyptian Sculpture Gallery. It involved a display of ancient artefacts, historic labels from the nineteenth century to the present day, and redundant gallery furniture from the museum's Department of Egyptian Antiquities, to address issues of acquisition history. This encompassed a photograph of a mummified human head mounted as if a taxidermy specimen, as well as the original display case for the Rosetta Stone with a new label addressing the visitor; 'what are you looking at?'. This, like his *Grey Area*, is a vital provocation for Egyptology, bringing emphasis to ideologies of seeing that operate within the museum. Such visual creations can themselves be considered theoretical frameworks, an 'interrogative archaeology', for museums (González 2001: 17) that can operate as a heuristic device based on discourse within, across, and beyond academia.

Despite these being more provocative interventions, they remain intermittent transgressions, sanctioned by museums that only briefly suspend their interpretive authority. Ultimately, museum representations usually revert to more orthodox narratives on a show's conclusion leaving little trace in the collection, its documentation, or the interpretive practice around it. The co-option of institutional critique within museological method in these instances acts as a release valve, easing tensions by seemingly addressing a controversy, but without seeking to seriously resolve them. The lack of such inscriptions has led many to criticize museums for their use of artists, who take on the effort of providing counter-narratives or responding to controversies while doing little to address their institutional structures (Geismar 2015). None of the *Time Machine* juxtapositions with British Museum objects are recorded in the publicly accessible database. To do so would anchor such transient framings within institutional memory, meaning that the curatorial intervention and academic citational practice could build on the artistic one, a critical observation if the museum is recognized as a site of experiment.

5.2 The Museum as Method

Thomas (2016) has suggested that creative work in museum collections is a method of research in its own right. Browsing through material is, he contends, a form of fieldwork as relationships between collections and archives are evaluated (discovery), words are put to objects (captioning), and objects are compared (juxtaposition). These processes, he argues, allow researchers to explore the fundamental categories that the comprise worldviews: The method is the use of the object in the exploration of what these categories and distinctions might mean, where they come from, where they mislead and where they remain useful or unavoidable. (Thomas 2016: 106)

For these reasons, several scholars have begun to frame museum activities as forms of experiment that create new perspectives and ideas (Bjerregaard 2019; Deliss 2012; MacDonald and Basu 2007). By conceptualizing the museum as laboratory, museum identities shift from being sites of hard stable truths, towards knowledge-producing locations, where objects and their frames are continuously questioned in dialogue with the world outside. These approaches can be useful for exploring both challenging histories and histories that are challenging to recover, such as in the case of work with small, longstanding, historically unprovenanced Egyptological collections of regional museums like that of Cyfarthfa Castle Museum and Art Gallery, Wales (Zinn 2019) or university collections such as the Haffenreffer Museum of Anthropology at Brown University (Thum and Troche 2016). In both cases, the public was invited to become part of interpretive projects using a range of techniques from the creative arts to the use of scientific instruments to develop insights and engagements with Egyptian artefacts. As noted earlier (Section 3.2) digital outputs are also increasingly being embraced and invested in as a means of connecting publics, researchers, and communities with collections and their documentation. Here too, experiments in blurring the distinctions between research and public outreach have been conducted. For example, MicroPasts, is a web-enabled crowd-sourcing project which allows for the collection and use of research data (Bonacchi et al. 2014). Projects have involved archival transcription of documents in the Egypt Exploration Society and geo-referencing tasks, as well as photomasking to support 3D object modelling, including of items in the Petrie Museum and Museo Egizo (Figure 20), facilitating research and extending it beyond the academy.

Figure 20 Screenshot of a Sketchfab image of a wooden shabti box of the steward of Djehutyhotep, New Kingdom, (1450–1350 BC). Old Fund 2443, Museo Egizio, Turin. Model available under Creative Commons BY 4.0 license (www.skfb.ly/XRHP), with thanks to Museo Egizio Turin and MicroPasts

The idea of experiment can further animate the idea of multi-directional curation and its applicability more broadly. Histories of collecting, material reproduction, relocation, and re-imagination might all be reassembled within an object biography, as has been popular in scholarship and museum practice for some time. Object biographies can be criticized for their additive linearity, although more complex relational networks that coalesce around objects have also been visualized on their basis (Byrne et al. 2011). Alternative approaches, such as object itineraries (Joyce and Gillespie 2015) have been also proffered, yet here too the model implies a singular trajectory which has be criticised for leading to recontextualizations that supplant and replace earlier moments in an object's life (Hicks 2021). This is not to say that the method ought to be rejected (contra Hicks 2021) since it retains enormous value in providing space for other voices and grassroots initiatives (Geismar 2021). Rather, a multi-directional approach can be seen as complementary, calling attention to the possibility for different times and places to be co-present, rather than organized sequentially – a composite structure which draws together into a single frame multiple moments and webs of signification (Silverman 2013: 3). This is important for museums, since as Ernst (2000) argued, museums are archives consisting of fragmented, dismembered, isolated, disfigured, and disjoined objects. The gap between the isolated presence of museum objects and their previous context-uality should not be blurred completely by interpolating narrative texts in the mode of the discourse of history. (Ernst 2000: 34)

Multi-directionality draws attention to this negotiation of fragmentary pasts in the present, highlighting as much the gaps, the overlaps, and disjunctions in interpretation as the connections. This is arguably a vital strategy for interpretative archaeology more generally, which is fundamentally self-reflexive and critically careful in its constructions of the past (e.g. Hodder 2000). There needs to be space for equivocation, ambiguity, and alternative possibilities, in place of assertive connoisseurship and authoritative statements which tend to be the mainstay of Egyptological display and treatise. This is not equivalent to absolute relativism, where anything goes, rather it is an act of interpretive maturity that is transparent about the unknowns and the evidential basis for claims. It leaves space for experimentation and for different registers of interpretive approach be they sculptures or academic prose. In other words, for acts of bricolage (Stevenson 2019: 243). In many respects this is what museums are already doing when they construct exhibitions; marshalling alternative media, voices, and commentary into the same space (Mao and Fu 2021). What multi-directionality foregrounds how-ever is how things that seem distantly related at first can be brought into dialogue; can be questioned and challenged from another perspective.

This is all well and good in theory. For museum professionals it poses considerable challenges. Time is one of the most difficult concepts to grasp in museums (van Broekhoven 2018: 74). Indeed, in the development of ancient Middle Eastern galleries at the Detroit Institute of Arts it was found that their first label drafts had reduced audience engagement as visitors became confused by the layering of multiple stories within the gallery (Anila and Emberling 2019: 135), while label word limits further constrain narrative possibilities. For such reasons, curators often rely on the seemingly intuitive timeline as an organizing framework for galleries and books. While useful, they can be taken for granted, presenting history as a path to the present. Timelines have further been critiqued for their linearity of narrative allowing space for just a single, fixed perspective (Lubar 2013). While museums have experimented with alternative formats, complete abandonment of timelines has faced fierce criticism. There are specific approaches that have been developed to address such issues, as in the British Museum, where evaluation of how visitors actually use galleries has led to the development of 'gateway objects' (Figure 21). This is an interpretive strategy focussed on single significant artefacts, the narration of which encompasses broader themes of relevance to whole galleries (Batty et al. 2016). This, potentially, has the advantage of shifting or indeed multiplying the *telos* of interpretation. The telos is 'the vantage point from which the past is envisaged' and which 'influences the selection of the material as well as its arrangement' (Grethlein 2014: 309). While the telos is the past for those interpreting today, for historical actors it is their future which may have been perceived and experienced differently in the absence of hindsight. What is considered significant or what is emphasized shifts with the telos, whether the narrative begins in the present, the recent past, or at any other historical points the object has born witness to.

Exhibitions are not created out of the ether, however. Museum collections management systems, through which exhibitions are frequently filtered, deserve closer attention as a means to experiment with and embrace the polysemic nature of objects. Rather than using new technologies to replicate old worldviews, there is potential to explore new configurations through alternative classifications and keywords that resonate with different times and places (Cameron 2005). Jones (2021) in his appraisal of the potential of artefacts, archives, and documentation, embraces metaphors not of networks, hierarchies, or trees, but of reefs, trails, and weaving, as a means of transcending approaches to artefacts pre-determined by sequence. He emphasizes relational documentation strategies that examine the associations between things, linking multiple classification systems simultaneously and building citations that connect objects with other informational repositories, be they photographs, replicas, samples, or publications. This necessitates, he argues, a slowing down, focussing upon how ideas are produced, circulated, and contextualized:

> If we fully accept the idea that museums are not neutral, embracing this approach represents a significant statement about what we see as important, prioritising the complex, relational nature of knowledge over efficiency, quantitative metrics, and institutional authority. (Jones 2021: 142)

Figure 21 An example of a 'gateway object', used as the introductory object for the National Museum of Scotland's Ancient Egypt gallery. © Alice Stevenson

5.3 Contemporary Collecting

In a multi-directional curatorial view, an object is subject to a spectrum of interpretive possibilities comprised of numerous inter-related experiences of making and remaking. If this is so, those other moments can be productively brought into dialogue with that object and may be evidenced by photographs, documents, oral histories, replicas, or modern artworks. For museums this might be achieved by raising the profile of other collection types so as to take them just as seriously as antiquities collections for curatorial care and institutional investment. Modern collections management standards usually require the production of development policies which situate current collection profiles under a museum's mission statement (or statement of purpose). Such documents identify themes and priorities for future collection, as well as for rationalization and disposal, all in the context of legal and ethical frameworks.[6] The establishment of these policies provides institutional commitment to new forms of collection mobilization. The 2019 Collections Development Policy for the University of Swansea's Egypt Centre, for instance, states that the museum 'may in future acquire items relating to the study of ancient Egypt, including artefacts from the pre-modern era, but also items relating to Egyptology such as photographs of sites, tourist souvenirs etc.'. The latter might be considered 'ephemera', deemed supplementary to exhibition themes. While owned by the museum in a legal sense, this is not the same as being 'accessioned' whereby this material is formally accepted into the primary collection where it is subject (in principle) to increased professional scrutiny, care, documentation, and public accessibility.

Policies matter to the discipline of Egyptology because they validate material and provide frameworks within which fresh approaches to the past and present can be achieved. It also highlights the role of contemporary collecting – not just collecting in the present but of the present – as one means to accommodate previously neglected perspectives on existing collections, as well as potentially experimentally addressing some of the silences in those collections. Given that museums outside of Egypt are not able to acquire antiquities from fieldwork as easily as in the past, and that the ethics of doing so are problematic, collecting efforts can be redirected elsewhere. Contemporary collecting is well developed in social history as a means of assembling material culture and stories connected to the recent past, or within 'living memory'. It can provide new contexts for existing collections and is undertaken in partnership with people and communities (Rhys and Baveystock 2014). There are well-known challenges to these approaches, including decisions on what is significant, whose voices and stories to include, who benefits, and how the material is made accessible in the long term. Those, however, are the very questions that Egyptology needs to ask of itself more broadly.

---

[6] See, for example, the Collections Trust Spectrum guidance: https://collectionstrust.org.uk/accredit ation/managing-collections/holding-and-developing-collections/collections-development-policy/ Similar guidance is provided by the American Alliance of Museums, and the International Council of Museums.

What sorts of materials might this include? New digital replicas, for instance, should be given serious consideration since they provide opportunities for others to repeat, expand, or critique previous experiments. Similar arguments have been made for the products of scientific sampling of museum objects (Quinn 2022), such as thin sections of ceramics. These usually remain with scientists as part of their own personal reference collections, but which are vulnerable to vagaries of professional life with no guarantee that those preparations will be retained if a laboratory closes or an academic retires. If accommodated within museum collections and documentation, there is a higher likelihood that they will be accessible for future research. A second reason for retention is that samples and replicas are also 'object lessons', 'ideas brought into being by things, not just as communication vehicles, but as sites of meaning *animated* by their materiality' (Geismar 2018: xv). There is already a tradition of replicas forming part of museum collections, from Pitt-Rivers' 1870s facsimile of a New Kingdom boomerang in the British Museum (Figure 22) to Randall-MacIver's 1907 recreations of Predynastic black-topped pottery (Stevenson 2015a). As forms of contemporary collecting these artefacts are embodiments of arguments latent with the potential for future dialogues that foreground assumptions around how the ancient past is known. If replicas or samples are formally acquired, their more recent histories and politics of acquisition still raise questions. They are predicated upon the command of technologies, itself a form of neo-colonization, especially when the technologies of production belong to corporations who exert copyright or ownership claims (Elias 2019).

Contemporary collecting could also be extended towards archaeological sites as a means of lending critical framing to current practices. Since the past is always produced in particular moments of interpretation, collecting around

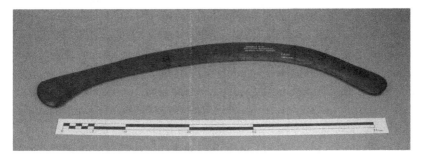

Figure 22 Facsimile of an Egyptian boomerang held by the British Museum made for experimentation by Pitt-Rivers in the 1870s and now in the collection of the Pitt Rivers Museum, Oxford (PRM 1884.25.30)

ongoing excavations has value in creating future interpretive aids, connecting past and present in new ways. Museums tend to contain historic photographic collections (see Section 3.1), but that freezes archaeology in particular times, unrepresentative of contemporary methods or issues. While publications, websites, and social media contain a profusion of fieldwork images, these are not generally collected by institutions in any systemic fashion. Such collecting would put the processes of fieldwork themselves under scrutiny. Digital objects should be subjected to similar modes of curatorial care as other types of things (Anderson et al. 2018).

Equally, this raises possibilities for collecting oral histories, as well as the soundscapes of fieldwork – labourers singing, calls to prayer (the *azan*), or the clanking of wheelbarrows. The Petrie Museum's archive, for instance, includes the notation of songs sung by Egyptian excavators during fieldwork (Quirke 2009: 439–61). Today, these are joined by recordings recently made in Egypt and which can be played at the entrance to the museum. Such interventions disrupt the kitsch ambience or Orientalized soundtracks that accompany TV documentaries and exhibitions, which situate Egyptian archaeology in Western discourse rather than the lived landscape of Egypt. These initiatives offer the chance to re-animate objects as part of human engagement and its environments (Krmpotich 2019), emphasizing the shared history that foreign archaeologists have with the Egyptians they work alongside, thereby re-humanizing the interpretive efforts of the discipline. This is not just a concern for museum representation, but a provocation to field archaeologists as well, underscoring fieldwork as a process of making shared history in the present.

These are not novel ideas, as they have been deployed in the design of projects at Çatalhöyük, Turkey (Hodder 2000) and Chichén Itzá, Mexico (Castañeda 2009), although less commonly are these initiatives placed into dialogue with museums as a concerted part of active collection policies. This does not just enhance displays. It may also be of methodological and moral significance in understanding archaeological site formation, as Lemos et al. (2017) have argued with regard to the excavation of Theban Tomb 187, a site demonstrating phases of reuse from ancient *and* modern times. Here, they argue, it is not the archaeologist's role to determine which periods of occupation are the most important since all potentially affect site deposition. Instead, their approach seeks to overcome the Orientalized biases of Egyptian archaeology that have dislocated local communities from the landscapes they have had a meaningful place within and places them in dialogue with, and as part of, the archaeological record. A second reason for taking sound seriously is due to developments in sensory archaeology, which recognizes that the past (like the present) was never silent. The full remit of ancient meaning making involves understanding the possibilities of landscapes and monuments to shape sensory experience and, in turn, the use and significance of those places (Butler and Nooter 2019). Wilfong's (2014) investigation of the sonic landscapes (not just music) of Karanis in Roman Egypt is one example. Acquiring sonic resources – be they experimental recordings of sounds in spaces, oral histories, or soundscapes of archaeological practice – means taking sound 'objects' (likely digital files) seriously as archaeological evidence for consultation and future evaluation, with all their implications for the format of long-term storage, appropriate meta-data needs, and display strategies (Levent et al. 2014).

Wesam Mohamed (2021) has offered another possibility for contemporary collecting, using pop-up exhibitions as 'laboratories' for collecting. At the Misr Public Library, Luxor, she initiated a co-curated exhibition, *El-Reis*, introducing Egyptian workmen as mediators between archaeology and local communities. Some 500 images were curated alongside personal possessions, the majority of which were brought by workmen themselves allowing alternative perspectives on the role of archaeology in Egypt, including debates around identity, postcolonialism, and antiquities protection. In these ways, contemporary collecting can bridge the gap between ancient and modern Egypt. Other strategies include collecting twentieth-century Egyptian material culture (Elshahed 2017), engaging modern Egyptian artists (Tully 2017), and including the voices and experiences of modern Egyptian communities in dialogue with collections and recorded in the relevant database records (Abd el-Gawad and Stevenson 2021). None of these are without their own issues; they still raise questions about representation, appropriation, and benefit. But what they provide are disruptions and intersections that can be generative for fresh research questions and presentations.

Where should these collections be housed? Given the rise of the post-digital museum, it is perhaps appropriate to consider a post-custodial archival model. The theory underpinning this posits that institutions no longer physically acquire material but instead offer management oversight while the archives themselves remain in the custody of record creators (Alpert-Abrams et al. 2019). Institutions, like the University of Texas Libraries (UTL), have developed programmes along these lines where they partner with organizations that seek to create and collect documentation, but who may lack resources or technical skills needed to preserve and access those materials. Within the partnership, collaborating groups maintain physical and intellectual custody over their materials while providing digital copies to UTL for long-term preservation and access. What is maintained in these arrangements is the sense that both UTL and the partner organizations have expertise that is shared towards a mutual goal of preservation and access. In theory, such a model when applied to Egypt might recognize a history of exploitation whereby archives have been removed from the country and redress is required, encouraging 'inclusive recording' (Mickel 2021) with Egyptian agency, while also providing opportunities to generate counter-narratives to those in conventional archives.[7]

There have, however, been previous attempts to subvert Western archival dominance over Egypt's past. In 1955, a documentation centre devoted to Egyptian archaeology was established as a collaboration between UNESCO and Egypt's Department of Antiquities – the Centre d'Étude et de Documentation sur l'Ancienne Égypte (CEDAE) – with an initial focus on the Aswan High Dam campaigns. Although founded in partnership, it remained steeped in colonial modes of recording orientated towards the Egyptian state's ongoing claims of sovereignty over Egypt's past. Carruthers (2020) has demonstrated how these concerns led in practice to some groups, such as Nubians, being ignored in favour of others, while access to the archives created is today severely restricted. Issues of copyright, general data protection regulation (GDPR), and other data privacy laws, as well as relationships to private industry, equally pose barriers to partnerships. Alienation from original contexts and sites of meaning-making remain, as they do with any acquired material. Whichever mode of collecting is adopted, the social conditions of knowledge production require continuous interrogation and it is likely that collections will still be shaped in unexpected, sometimes unwanted, ways. Time will tell.

6 Concluding Remarks

This Element opened with the British Museum's *A History of the World in 100 Objects*. Ten years on, a new initiative sought to return to, critique, and move beyond it, challenging the premise that the museum could be a place to see the world without any reflection on how the institution itself acquired and reframed objects in order to create its own seemingly universal narrative. The project's title, *A 100 Histories of a 100 Worlds in One Object*,[8] signalled the multiplicity of directions in which histories could be implicated. One of the first artefacts tackled was the Rosetta Stone. Amongst the world's most iconic museum objects, the Stone's well-known narrative of decipherment has led the name 'Rosetta' to transcend its Egyptian and Egyptological context. The image of the three scripts on its surface is similarly recognized globally and is central to the British Museum's branding. Pictures of the fourth script on the stone's surface

---

[7] Egyptian examples outside of Egyptology and archaeology include Shubra archive (https://twitter .com/sard_shubra) and Egypt migrations (https://egyptmigrations.com/)
[8] https://100histories100worlds.org/

are less widely circulated; etched in large typeface on the left side 'captured in Egypt by the British Army in 1801', 'presented by King George III' on the right. Several histories are materialized by this single stela, ones that are not separate, not competing, but dialogically related. For the Egyptian narrator of this history, Abd el-Gawad (2020), 'Rosetta' resonated not just with Egyptology's history, but with a specific landscape and its inhabitants; the port and people of Rashid in the Egyptian Delta from where the artefact was wrested by the French army. While repatriation debates engulf this object, rarely, Abd el-Gawad notes, do they consider how communities in Rashid might benefit from or be emancipated in these histories.

The arguments developed in this Element are predicated on the fact that artefacts, documents, photographs, replicas, and digital objects all make multiple pasts manifest in the present. Implicitly or explicitly, they have a direct bearing on how the past is narrated and how it is perceived from the present. A multi-directional approach potentially illuminates these overlapping relations between semi-autonomous layers of time. This does then beg the question of how historical representations gain legitimacy and social relevance. It is, therefore, imperative to reflect upon the constituents that comprise evidential claims; processes and contexts of collection, documentation, replication, location, and experiment. In order to develop these critical skills, working with historic collections (in the fullest sense of object and archive) should be part of all Egyptological and archaeological training to cultivate a sensitivity to how ideas are produced. This might ensure that future fieldworkers are consciously aware of how their practices stand up to historical examination and what resources are needed to enfranchise fresh forms of knowledge production, whether through contemporary collecting or post-custodial archiving. Such a project can never be complete, but perhaps it will provide further fragments through which alternative pasts and futures may yet be (re)assembled.

References

Abd el-Gawad, H. 2020. Re(claiming) the Rosetta: The Rosetta stone and the (re)writing of Egypt's modern history. *100 Histories of 100 Worlds in One Object*. https://100histories100worlds.org/reclaiming-the-rosetta/ [Accessed 21 December 2021]

Abd el-Gawad, H. and Stevenson, A. 2021. Egypt's dispersed heritage: Using comic art for multidirectional storytelling. *Journal of Social Archaeology* 21 (1): 121–45.

Abd el-Gawad, H. and Stevenson, A. In press. Egyptian mummified remains: Source community perspectives. In Clary, K. S. and Biers, T. (eds.) *Museums, Heritage and Death*. London: Routledge.

Adams, B. 1993. Potmark forgery: a serekh of Semerkhet from Abydos. *Discussions in Egyptology* 25: 1–12.

Aïdi, H. 2022. Egypt and the Afrocentrists: The latest round. *Africa is a Country*, 23 March. https://africasacountry.com/2022/03/egypt-and-the-afrocentrists-the-latest-round [Accessed 3 April 2022]

Al-Azm, A. and Paul, K. A. 2019. Facebook's black market in antiquities: Trafficking, terrorism, and war crimes. *ATHAR Project*. http://atharproject .org/wp-content/uploads/2019/06/ATHAR-FB-Report-June-2019-final.pdf [Accessed 21 December 2021]

Alberro, A. 2009. Institutions, critique, and institutional critique. In Alberro, A. and Stimson, B. (eds.) *Institutional Critique: An Anthology of Artists' Writings*. Cambridge, MA: MIT Press, 2–19.

Alberti, S. 2005. Objects and the museum. *Isis* 96(4): 559–71.

Alpert-Abrams, H., Bliss, D. A. and Carbajal, I. 2019. Post-custodialism for the collective good: Examining neoliberalism in US-Latin American archival part-nerships, in evidences, implications, and critical interrogations of neoliberalism in information studies. *Journal of Critical Library and Information Studies* 2(1): 1–24.

Ambridge, L. 2012. Imperialism and racial geography in James Henry Breasted's 'Ancient Times, a History of the Early World'. *Journal of Egyptian History* 5: 12–33.

Amico, N., Ronzino, P., Vassallo, V. et al. 2018. Theorizing authenticity, practis-ing reality: The 3D replica of the Kazaphani boat. In Di Giuseppantonio Di Franco, P., Galeazzi, F. and Vassallo, V. (eds.) *Authenticity and Cultural Heritage in the Age of 3D Digital Reproductions*. Cambridge: McDonald Institute, 111–22.

Anderson, H., Galvin, E. and Rodriguez, J. de T. 2018. Museological approaches to the management of digital research and engagement: The African rock art image project. *African Archaeological Review* 35: 321–37.

Anila, S. and Emberling, G. 2019. Negotiations in museum practice. In Emberling, G. and Petit, L. P. (eds.) *Museums and the Ancient Middle East: Curatorial Practices*. London: Routledge, 123–37.

Asante, M. K. 1995. *Kemet, Afrocentricity and Knowledge*. Eritrea: African World Press.

Ashcroft, B., Griffiths, G. and Tiffin, H. 2000. *Post-Colonial Studies: The Key Concepts*. London: Routledge.

Ashton, S.-A. 2011. Curating Kemet, fear of a black-land? In Exell, K. (ed.) *Egypt in its African Context*. Oxford: BAR, 105–14.

Azoulay, A. A. 2019. *Potential History: Unlearning Imperialism*. London: Verso.

Baird, J. 2020. Time, objectivity and the archive. In McFadyen, L. and Hicks, D. (eds.) *Archaeology and Photography*. London: Routledge, 73–95.

Bakhtin, M. M. 1981. *The Dialogic Imagination: Four Essays*. Austin: University of Texas Press.

Barker, E. 1999. Introduction. In Barker, E. (ed.) *Contemporary Cultures of Display*. New Haven: Yale University Press, 8–21.

Barker, M. 2010. The reproductive continuum: Plaster casts, paper mosaics and photographs as complementary modes of reproduction in the nineteenth-century museum. In Frederiksen, R. and Marchand, E. (eds.) *Plaster Casts: Making, Collecting and Displaying from Classical Antiquity to the Present*. Berlin: De Gruyter, 485–500.

Batty, J., Carr, J., Edwards, C. et al. 2016. Object-focused text at the British Museum. *Exhibition* 36(1): 71–80.

Bennett, T. 1995. *The Birth of the Museum*. London: Routledge.

Bjerregaard, P. (ed.) 2019. *Exhibitions as Research: Experimental Methods in Museums*. London: Routledge.

Blackman, W. S. 1927. *The Fellahin of Upper Egypt: Their Religious, Social and Industrial Life To-day with Special Reference to Survivals from Ancient Times*. London: Harrap.

Boast, R. and Enote, J. 2013. Virtual repatriation: It is neither virtual nor repatriation. In Biehl, P. F. and Prescott, C. (eds.) *Heritage in the Context of Globalization: Europe and the Americas*. New York: Springer, 103–13.

Bodenstein, F. 2012. Framing the artifact: Murals for the display of antiquity in the Louvre. *Museum History Journal* 5(2): 167–86.

Bohrer, F. N. 2011. *Photography and Archaeology*. London: Reaktion.

Bonacchi, C., Bevan, A., Pett, D. et al. 2014. Crowd-sourced archaeological research: The MicroPasts project. *Archaeology International* 17: 61–8.

Boozer, A. 2015. The tyranny of typologies: Evidential reasoning in Romano-Egyptian domestic architecture. In Chapman, R. and Wylie, A. (eds.) *Material Evidence: Learning from Archaeological Practice.* London: Routledge, 92–110.

Borriello, M. R. and Giove, T. 2000. *The Egyptian Collection of the National Archaeological Museum of Naples.* Naples: Electa Napoli.

Bourriau, J. and Quirke, S. 1988. *Pharaohs and Mortals: Egyptian Art in the Middle Kingdom.* Cambridge: Cambridge University Press.

Brancaglion, A. 2018. Egypt in Rio: The national museum lives. *CiPEG News* 10: 2.

Bresciani, E. and Betrò, M. (eds.) 2004. *Egypt in India: Egyptian Antiquities in Indian Museums.* Pisa: Pisa University Press, 63–71.

Brodie, N. 2017. The role of conservators in facilitating the theft and trafficking of cultural objects: The case of a seized Libyan statue. *Libyan Studies* 48: 117–23.

Brusius, M. 2017. The field in the museum: Puzzling out Babylon in Berlin. *Osiris* 32(1): 264–85.

Brusius, M. and Singh, K. 2017. Introduction. In Singh, K. and Brusius, M. (eds.) *Museum Storage and Meaning: Tales from the Crypt.* London: Routledge, 1–33.

Butler, S. and Nooter, S. (eds.) 2019. *Sound and the Ancient Senses.* London: Routledge.

Byrne, S., Clarke, A., Harrison, R. and Torrence, R. 2011. Networks, agents and objects: Frameworks for unpacking museum collections. In Byrne, S., Clarke, A., Harrison, R. and Torrence, R. (eds.) *Unpacking the Collection: Networks of Material and Social Agency in the Museum.* New York: Springer, 3–26.

Cafici, G. 2021. Rediscovering the nineteenth-century display of the Museum Egizio's 'Satuario'. *Rivista del Museo Egizio* 5: 57–86. https://doi.org/10.29353/rime.2021.3720

Cameron, F. 2005. Museum collections, documentation, and shifting knowledge paradigms. *Collections: A Journal for Museum and Archive Professionals* 1(3): 243–59.

Capel, A. K. and Markoe, G. (eds.) 1996. *Mistress of the House, Mistress of Heaven: Women in Ancient Egypt.* New York: Hudson Hill Press.

Carruthers, W. 2014. Introduction. In Carruthers, W. (ed.) *Histories of Egyptology.* London: Routledge, 1–18.

Carruthers, W. 2020. Records of dispossession: Archival thinking and UNESCO's Nubian campaign in Egypt and Sudan. *International Journal of Islamic Architecture* 9(2): 287–324.

Carruthers, W. 2021. Spectacles of the past. *Jadaliyya*, 12 May. www.jadaliyya.com/Details/42719/Spectacles-of-the-Past

Castañeda, Q. E. 2009. The 'past' as transcultural space: Using ethnographic installation in the study of archaeology. *Public Archaeology* 8(2–3): 262–82.

Challis, D. 2013. *The Archaeology of Race: The Eugenic Ideas of Francis Galton and Flinders Petrie.* London: Bloomsbury.

Chapman, R. and Wiley, A. 2016. *Evidential Reasoning in Archaeology.* London: Bloomsbury.

Chudzik, P. 2017. *The Art of Ancient Egypt, the Collection of Plaster Casts at the University of Wroclaw, the Treasures of University Collections.* Wroclaw: University of Wroclaw.

Claes, W., De Meyer, M., Gräzer, O. A. and Van der Perre, A. 2021. Sura-project van start: Egypte door een fotografische lens. *FARO: Tijdschrift over cultureel erfgoed* 14(1): 46–9.

Clarysse, W. and Yan, H. 2006. Antiquités égyptiennes à Pékin. *Competes rendus des séances de l'Académie des Inscriptions et Belles-Lettres* 150(2): 833–9.

Clifford, J. 2019. The times of the curator. In Schorch, P. and McCarthy, C. (eds.) *Curatopia: Museums and the Future of Curatorship.* Manchester: Manchester University Press, 109–23.

Colla, E. 2007. *Conflicted Antiquities: Egyptology, Egyptomania, Egyptian Modernity.* Durham: Duke University Press.

Coombes, R. and Phillips, R. (eds.) 2020. *Museum Transformations: Decolonization and Democratization.* Chichester: Wiley-Blackwell.

Cooper, C. 2019. You can handle it: 3D printing for museums. *Advances in Archaeological Practice* 7(4): 443–7.

Coote, J. 2012. Objects and words: Writing on, around, and about things – an introduction. *Journal of Museum Ethnography* 25: 3–18.

Crane, S. A. 2000. Introduction: Of museums and memory. In Crane, S. A. (ed.) *Museums and Memory.* Palo Alto: Stanford University Press, 1–17.

Crane, S. A. 2008. The conundrum of ephemerality: Time, memory, and museums. In Macdonald, S. (ed.) *A Companion to Museum Studies.* Hoboken: Wiley-Blackwell, 98–109.

Cummins, E. 2016. A curatorial dilemma: An examination of temporary exhibitions combining African and Egyptian visual culture. *Journal of Ancient Egyptian Interconnections* 8: 21–5.

Davies, V. 2019–20. W. E. B. Du Bois, a new voice in Egyptology's disciplinary history. *Ankh* 28(29): 19–29.

Dawson, A. 2016. Outcry after Toledo Museum of Art sells ancient Greek and Egyptian objects at auction. *The Art Newspaper,* 5 November. https://www.theartnewspaper.com/2016/11/05/outcry-after-toledo-museum-of-art-sells-ancient-greek-and-egyptian-objects-at-auction [Accessed 16 June 2022].

Day, J. 2006. *The Mummy's Curse: Mummymania in the English-Speaking World*. London: Routledge.

Del Vesco, P. 2022. Engaging contemporary social issues in the museum through archaeological collections. In Stevenson, A. (ed.) *The Oxford Handbook of Museum Archaeology*. Oxford: Oxford University Press, 503–25.

Del Vesco, P. and Moiso, B. (eds.) 2017. *Missione Egitto 1903–1920: L'avventura archeologica M. A. I raccontata*. Turin: Museo Egizio.

Deliss, C. 2012. *Object Atlas: Fieldwork in the Museum*. Frankfurt am Main: Kerber.

Desvallées, A., de Bary, M.-O. and Wasserman, F. 1992. *Vagues, une anthologie de la nouvelle muséologie*. 2 vols. Mâcon: éditions W, Savigny-le-Temple, M.N.E.S.

Doyon, W. 2008. The poetics of Egyptian museum practice. *British Museum Studies in Ancient Egypt and Sudan* 10: 1–37.

Doyon, W. 2018. The history of archaeology through the eyes of Egyptians. In Effros, B. and Lai, G. (eds.) *Unmasking Ideology in Imperial and Colonial Archaeology*. Los Angeles: Cotsen Institute of Archaeology Press, 173–200.

Driver, F., Nesbitt, M., and Cornish, C. 2021. Introduction: Mobilising and re-mobilising museum collections. In Driver, F., Nesbitt, M., and Cornish, C. (eds.) *Mobile Museums. Collections in Circulation*. London: UCL Press, 1–20.

Du Bois, W. E. B. 1947. *The World and Africa*. New York: The Viking Press.

Duncan, C. 1995. *Civilizing Rituals: Inside Public Art Museums*. London: Routledge.

Edwards, A. 1877. *A Thousand Miles Up the Nile*. London: Longmans.

Edwards, E. 2010. Photographs and history: Emotion and materiality. In Dudley, S. (ed.) *Museum Materialities: Objects, Engagements, Interpretations*. London: Routledge, 21–38.

Edwards, E. 2019. What are photographs doing in museums? *V&A Blog*, 3 December. www.vam.ac.uk/blog/museum-life/what-are-photographs-doing-in-museums [Accessed 21 December 2021]

Edwards, E. and Lien, S. 2014. Introduction: Museums and the work of photographs. In Edwards, E. and Lien, S. (eds.) *Uncertain Images: Museums and the Work of Photographs*. London: Routledge, 3–20.

Edwards, E. and Morton, C. 2015. Between art and information: Towards a collecting history of photographs. In Edwards, E. and Morton, C. (eds.) *Photographs, Museums, Collections: Between Art and Information*. London: Bloomsbury Academic, 3–23.

Eissa, M. and el-Senussi, A. 2020. Egyptian museums and storehouses. In Shaw, I. and Bloxam, E. (eds.) *The Oxford Handbook of Egyptology*. Oxford: Oxford University Press, 1185–202.

El Nagar, A. and Derbali, A. M. S. 2020. The importance of tourism contributions in Egyptian economy. *International Journal of Hospitality and Travel* 1 (1): 45–52.

el-Moniem, A. 2005. The national museum of Egyptian civilization. *Museum International* 57(1-2): 24–30.

Elias, C. 2019. Whose digital heritage? Contemporary art, 3D printing and limits of cultural property. *Third Text* 33(6): 687–707.

Elnaggar, A. 2014. Storage issues in Egyptian heritage: Risk assessment, conservation needs and policy planning. *Egyptological Documents, Archives, Libraries* 4: 155–64.

Elnozahy, M. 2021. Forever is now, on the art of Art D'Égypte. *Mada Masr*, 20 October. https://mada31.appspot.com/www.madamasr.com/en/2021/10/20/feature/culture/forever-is-now-on-the-art-of-art-degypte/#footnote-1 [Accessed 14 January 2022].

Elshahed, M. 2015. The old and new Egyptian museums. In Carruthers, W. (ed.) *Histories of Egyptology*. London: Routledge, 255–69.

Elshahed, M. 2017. Collecting modern Egypt. *British Museum Blog*. https://blog.britishmuseum.org/collecting-modern-egypt/ [Accessed 11 November 2021]

Emberling, G. 2020. Exhibiting ancient Africa at the Museum of Fine Arts, Boston: 'Ancient Nubia Now' and its audiences. *American Journal of Archaeology* 124(3): 511–19.

Ernst, W. 2000. Archi(ve) textures of museology. In Crane, S. A. (ed.) *Museums and Memory*. Palo Alton: Stanford University Press, 17–34.

Fabian, J. 1983. *Time and the Other: How Anthropology Makes its Object*. New York: Columbia University Press.

Fazzini, R. A. 1995. Presenting Egyptian objects: Concepts and approaches. *Museum International* 47(2): 38–43.

Fedi, M. E., Caforio, L., Liccioli, L. et al. 2014. A simple and effective removal procedure of synthetic resins to obtain accurate radiocarbon dates of restored artworks. *Radiocarbon* 56(3): 969–79.

Fletcher, R. 2012. The art of forgetting: Imperialist amnesia and public secrecy. *Third World Quarterly* 33(3): 423–39.

Foster, S. 1982. The exotic as a symbolic system. *Dialogical Anthropology* 7: 21–30.

Foster, S. and Curtis, N. 2016. The thing about replicas. *European Journal of Archaeology* 19(1): 122–48.

Foucault, M. 1972. *The Archaeology of Knowledge and the Discourse on Language*. Translated from the French by A. M. Sheridan Smith. New York: Pantheon Books.

Franzmeier, H. 2021. '. . . half a loaf is better than no bread': On the fragmentary nature of early archaeological publications and their utilisation in the 21st century. In Kilian, A. and Zöller-Engelhardt, M. (eds.) *Excavating the Extra-Ordinary: Challenges and Merits of Working with Small Finds*. Heidelberg: Propylaeum, 71–97.

Funari, P. P. A. and Funari, R. S. 2010. Ancient Egypt in Brazil: A theoretical approach to contemporary uses of the past. *Archaeologies* 6: 48–61.

Galán, J. M. and Menéndez, G. 2011. The funerary banquet of Hery (TT12), robbed and restored. *Journal of Egyptian Archaeology* 97: 143–66.

Gänsicke, S., Hatchfield, P., Hykin, A., Svoboda, M. and Mei-An Tsu, C. 2003. The ancient Egyptian collection at the Museum of Fine Arts, Boston: Part 2, A review of former treatments at the MFA and their consequences. *Journal of the American Institute for Conservation* 42(2): 193–236.

Geismar, H. 2015. The art of anthropology: Questioning contemporary art in ethnographic display. In Message, K. and Witcomb, A. (eds.) *The International Handbook of Museum Studies: Museum Theory*. Malden: Blackwell, 183–210.

Geismar, H. 2018. *Museum Object Lessons for the Digital Age*. London: UCL Press.

Geismar, H. 2021. In defence of the object biography. *British Art Studies* 19. https://doi.org/10.17658/issn.2058-5462/issue-19/conversation

Gell, A. 1992. The technology of enchantment and the enchantment of technology. In Coote, J. and Shelton, A. (eds.) *Anthropology, Art and Aesthetics*. Oxford: Clarendon Press, 40–63.

Gerstenblith, P. 2019. Provenances: Real, fake, and questionable. *International Journal of Cultural Property* 26(3): 285–304.

Gertzen, T. 2021. Some remarks on the 'de-colonization' of Egyptology. *Göttinger Miszellen* 261: 189–203.

González, J. 2001. Against the grain: The artist as conceptual materialist. In Berger, M. (ed.) *Fred Wilson: Object and Installations 1979–2000*. Baltimore: University of Maryland, 22–31.

Grethlein, J. 2014. 'Future past': Time and teleology in (ancient) historiography. *History and Theory* 53: 309–30.

Guha, S. 2013. Beyond representations: Photographs in archaeological knowledge. *Complutum* 24: 173–88.

Hagen, F. and Ryholt, K. 2016. *The Antiquities Trade in Egypt 1880–1930: The H.O. Lange Papers*. Copenhagen: Royal Danish Academy of Science and Letters.

Hamdan, G. al-Din. 1967. *Shakhsiat Misr (The Personality of Egypt)*. Cairo: Kitab al-Hilal [in Arabic].

Hanna, M. 2016. Documenting looting activities in post-2011 Egypt. In Desmarais, F. (ed.) *Countering Illicit Traffic in Cultural Goods: The Global Challenge of Protecting the World's Heritage*. Paris: International Council of Museums, 47–64.

Harrington, N. 2018. A world without play? Children in ancient Egyptian art and iconography. In Crawford, S., Hadley, D. M. and Shepherd, G. (eds.) *The Oxford Handbook of the Archaeology of Childhood*. Oxford: Oxford University Press, 539–556.

Harris, O. J. T. 2021. Archaeology, process and time: Beyond history versus memory. *World Archaeology* 53(1): 104–21.

Hassanein, M. and Kamal, F. 2021. The new Sharm el-Sheikh museum and its role in cultural tourism. *CiPEG e-News* 15: 2.

Heneghan Peng Architects. n.d. The Grand Egyptian Museum, Giza, Egypt. *Heneghan Peng Architects*. www.hparc.com/work/the-grand-egyptian-museum/ [Accessed 6 April 2022]

Hicks, D. 2021. Necrography: Death-writing in the colonial museum. *British Art Studies* 19. https://doi.org/10.17658/issn.2058-5462/issue-19/conversation

Hodder, I. (ed.) 2000. *Towards Reflexive Method in Archaeology*. Cambridge: McDonald Institute for Archaeological Research.

Hodjash, S. 1995. Ancient Egypt in Russia, Ukraine, the Caucasus, the Baltics and Central Asia. *Museum International* 47(2): 33–7.

Hoffman, M. 1979. *Egypt before the Pharaohs*. New York: Knopf.

Holdaway, S., Emmit, J. and Phillipps, R. 2022. Recreating context for museum collections using digital technologies as a form of curation. In Stevenson, A. (ed.) *The Oxford Handbook of Museum Archaeology*. Oxford: Oxford University Press, 353–73.

Holtorf, C. 2013. On pastness: A reconsideration of materiality in archaeological object authenticity. *Anthropological Quarterly* 86: 427–43.

Hooper-Greenhill, E. 1992. *Museums and the Interpretation of Visual Culture*. London: Routledge.

Howard, D. M., Schofield, J., Fletcher, J. et al. 2020. Synthesis of a vocal sound from the 3,000 year old mummy, Nesyamun 'true of voice'. *Nature: Scientific Reports*, 23 January. www.nature.com/articles/s41598-019-56316-y [Accessed 21 December 2021]

Howley, K. 2020. The materiality of shabtis: Figurines over four millennia. *Cambridge Archaeological Journal* 30(1): 123–40.

Hurley, C. 2020. Pharaohs, papyri and hookahs: Displaying and staging Egyptian antiquities in nineteenth century European exhibitions. In Versluys, M. J. (ed.) *Beyond Egyptomania: Objects, Style and Agency*. Berlin: De Gruyter, 185–208.

ICOM 2017. *ICOM Code of Ethics for Museums*. Paris: International Council of Museums.

Jarsaillon, C. 2017. Schiaparelli et les archéologues italiens aux bords du Nil: égyptologie et rivalités diplomatiques entre 1882 et 1922. *Rivista del Museo Egizio* 1: 87–107. https://doi.org/10.29353/rime.2017.1231

Jenkins, D. 1994. Object lessons and ethnographic displays: Museum exhibitions and the making of American anthropology. *Comparative Studies in Society and History* 26(2): 242–70.

Johnson, J. 2021. Dirty hands: Assessing Egyptology's racist past in the age of Black Lives Matter. *The Thinking Republic*, March. www.thethinkingrepublic .com/fulcrum/dirty-hands [Accessed 20 December 2021]

Jones, M. 2021. *Artefacts, Archives, and Documentation in the Relational Museum*. London: Routledge.

Joyce, R. and Gillespie, S. D. (eds.) 2015. *Things in Motion: Object Itineraries in Anthropological Practice*. Santa Fe: SAR Press.

Joyeux-Prunel, B. and Marcel, O. 2015. Exhibition catalogues in the globalization of art: A source for social and spatial art history. *Artl@s Bulletin* 4(2): article 8.

Kaeser, M.-A. (ed.) 2011. *L'âge du Faux: L'authenticité en archéologie*. Hauterive: Laténium.

Kaplan, F. E. S. 1995. *Museums and the Making of 'Ourselves'*. London: Leicester University Press.

Karp, I. and Kratz, C. A. 2014. Collecting, exhibiting, and interpreting: Museums as mediators and midwives of meaning. *Museum Anthropology* 37(1): 51–65.

Kersel, M. 2015. Storage wars: Solving the archaeological curation crisis? *Journal of Eastern Mediterranean Archaeology and Heritage Studies* 3(1): 42–54.

Klamm, S. 2015. Retusche, Zensur und Manipulation – Gedruckte Fotografie im Ersten Weltkrieg. In Ziehe, I. and Hägele, U. (eds.) *Gedruckte Fotografie: Abbild, Objekt und mediales Format*. Münster: Waxmann, 45–55.

Knell, S. 2019. Introduction: The museum in the global contemporary. In Knell, S (ed.) *The Contemporary Museum: Shaping Museums for the Global Now*. London: Routledge, 1–10.

Kreiter, R. P. 2020. Conceptualizing the past in museum exhibitions of ancient Egyptian and Near Eastern Art. In Gansell, A. and Shafer, A. (eds.) *Testing the Canon of Ancient Near Eastern Art and Archaeology*. Oxford: Oxford University Press, 253–73.

Křížová, M. 2021. Curators, objects and the indigenous agency. *Reviews in Anthropology* 50(1–2): 22–40.

Krmpotich, C. 2019. The sense in museums: Knowledge production, democratization and indigenization. In Skeates, R. and Day, J. (eds.) *The Routledge Handbook of Sensory Archaeology*. London: Routledge, 94–106.

Krstović, N. 2020. Colonizing knowledge: New museology as museology of news. *Prace Etnograficzne* 49(2): 125–39.

La, K. C. 2011. Object to project: Artists' interventions in museum collections. In Marshall, S. (ed.) *Sculpture and the Museum*. Farnham: Ashgate, 216–39.

Lavrentyeva, N. V. 2017. Re-birth of an Egyptian statue: Unfolding a network through time and space. *CiPEG Journal* 1: 35–44.

Lehrer, E. 2020. Material Kin: 'Communities of implication' in post-colonial, post-holocaust polish ethnographic collections. In von Oswald, M. and Tinius, J. (eds.) *Across Anthropology: Troubling Colonial Legacies, Museums, and the Curatorial*. Leuven: Leuven University Press, 289–323.

Lemos, R., Seehausen, P. L. von, Giovanni, M. D. et al. 2017. Entangled temporalities in the Theban necropolis: A materiality and heritage approach to the excavation of Theban Tomb 187. *Journal of Eastern Mediterranean Archaeology and Heritage Studies* 5(2): 178–97.

Levent, N. S., Pascual-Leone, A. and Lacey, S. (eds.) 2014. *The Multisensory Museum: Cross-Disciplinary Perspectives on Touch, Sound, Smell, Memory, and Space*. Lanham: Rowman & Littlefield.

Levitt, P. and Parrs, A. 2019. Hiding in plain sight: The Coptic Museum in the Egyptian cultural landscape. *International Journal of Cultural Policy* 25(6): 653–66.

Lilyquist, C. 1988. The gold bowl naming General Djehuty: A study of objects and early Egyptology. *Metropolitan Museum Journal* 23: 5–68.

Lilyquist, C. 2003. *The Tomb of Three Foreign Wives of Thutmosis III*. New York: Metropolitan Museum of Art.

Lipson, C. 2013. Comparative rhetoric, Egyptology, and the case of Akhenaten. *Rhetoric Society Quarterly* 43(3): 270–84.

Livingstone, D. 2003. *Putting Science in its Place: Geographies of Scientific Knowledge*. Chicago: Chicago University Press.

Lubar, S. 2013. Timelines in exhibitions. *Curator* 56(2): 169–88.

MacDonald, S. and Basu, P. (ed.) 2007. *Exhibition Experiments*. Oxford: Blackwell.

MacGregor, A. 2007. *Curiosity and the Enlightenment: Collectors and Collections from the Sixteenth to the Nineteenth Century*. New Haven: Yale University Press.

MacGregor, N. 2010. *A History of the World in 100 Objects*. London: Penguin.

Mackenzie, S., Brodie, N., Yates, D. and Tsirogiannis, C. 2019. *Trafficking Culture: New Directions in Researching the Global Market in Illicit Antiquities.* London: Routledge.

MacLeod, S. 2005. *Reshaping Museum Space: Architecture, Design, Exhibitions.* London: Routledge.

Mairesse, F. 2019. The definition of the museum: History and issues. *Museum International* 71: 154–9.

Manuelian, P. D. 2015. Harvard University-Boston Museum of Fine Art expedition contributions to Old Kingdom history at Giza: Some rights and wrongs. In Manuelian, P. D. and Schneider, T. (eds.) *Towards a New History for the Egyptian Old Kingdom: Perspectives on the Pyramid Age.* Leiden: Brill, 315–36.

Mao, R. and Fu, Y. 2021. Interweaving multiple contexts for objects in museum exhibitions: A contextual approach. *Museum Management and Curatorship.* https://doi.org/10.1080/09647775.2021.1914141

Marchand, S. 2015. The dialectics of the antiquities rush. In Fenet, A. and Lubtchansky, N. (eds.) *Pour une historie de l'archéologie XVIII siècle–1945: Hommage de ses collègues et amis à Ève Gran-Aymerich.* Pesac: Ausonius Èditions, 191–206.

Maspero, G. 1912. *Rapports sur la marche du Service des Antiquités, de 1899 à 1910.* Cairo: Imprimerie Nationale.

Matić, U. 2020. *Ethnic Identities in the Land of the Pharaohs.* Cambridge: Cambridge University Press.

Meleounis, D. 2009. Managing early museum collections of ancient Egyptian materials. MA Thesis, Seton Hall University. https://scholarship.shu.edu/theses/250

Merriman, N. 2004. Involving the public museum archaeology. In Merriman, N. (ed.) *Public Archaeology.* London: Routledge, 85–108.

Meskell, L. 2004. *Object Worlds in Ancient Egypt: Material Biographies Past and Present.* Oxford: Berg.

Mickel, A. 2021. *Why Those Who Shovel Are Silent: The Unknown Experts of Archaeological Excavation.* Lousiville: University Press of Colorado.

Miniaci, G. 2020. Global history in Egyptology: Framing resilient shores. *Journal of Egyptian History* 13: 409–21.

Minor, E. 2018. Decolonizing Reisner: A case study of a Classic Kerma female burial for reinterpreting early Nubian archaeological collections through digital archival resources. In Honegger, M. (ed.) *Nubian Archaeology in the XXIst Century: Proceedings of the Thirteenth International Conference for Nubian Studies.* Leuven: Peeters, 251–62.

Minott, R. 2019. The past is now: Confronting museums' complicity in imperial celebration. *Third Text* 33(4/5): 559–74.

Modest, W. and Lelijveld, R. (eds.) 2018. *Words Matter: An Unfinished Guide to Word Choices in the Cultural Sector*. Amsterdam: National Museum of World Cultures.

Mohamed, W. 2021. El-Reis: Co-curated exhibition. *CiPEG News* 16: 5.

Montserrat, D. 1996. 'No papyrus and no portraits': Hogarth, Grenfell and the first season in the Fayum, 1895–96. *Bulletin of the American Society of Papyrologists* 33: 133–76.

Montserrat, D. 2000. *Akhenaten: History, Fantasy and Ancient Egypt*. London: Routledge, 68–9.

Morfini, I. 2016. An Egyptian collection held in the National Museum in Accra. *Göttinger Miszellen* 249: 125–9.

Morphy, H. 2015. The displaced local: Multiple agency in the building of museums ethnographic collections. In Message, K. and Witcomb, A. (eds.) *The International Handbook of Museum Studies: Museum Theory*. Oxford: Wiley-Blackwell, 365–86.

Moser, S. 2006. *Wondrous Curiosities: Ancient Egypt at the British Museum*. Chicago: University of Chicago Press.

Moser, S. 2008. Archaeological representation: The consumption and creation of the past. In Cunliffe, B. and Gosden, C. (eds.) *The Oxford Handbook of Archaeology*. Oxford: Oxford University Press, 1048–77.

Moser, S. 2010. The devil is in the detail: Museum displays and the creation of knowledge. *Museum Anthropology* 33(1): 22–32.

Moser, S. 2019. *Painting Antiquity: Egypt in the Art of Lawrence Alma-Tadema, Edward Poynter and Edwin Long*. Oxford: Oxford University Press.

Moser, S. and Nicola, G. L. 2017. Sharing knowledge for restoring coffins: The case of Civico Museo di Storia e Arte of Trieste. In Amenta, A. and Guichard, H. (eds.) *Proceedings First Vatican Coffin Conference*. Vatican City: Edizioni Musei Vaticani, 317–26.

Muñiz-Reed, I. 2017. Thoughts on curatorial practices in the decoloninal turn. *OnCurating* 35: 99–105.

Nyord, R. 2018. Taking ancient Egyptian mortuary religion seriously: Why would we, and how could we? *Journal of Ancient Egyptian Interconnections* 17: 73–87.

O'Connell, E. 2014. The discovery of Christian Egypt: From manuscript hunters toward an archaeology of the late Antique Egypt. In Gabra, G. (ed.) *Coptic Civilization: Two Thousand Years of Christianity in Egypt*. Cairo: AUC Press, 163–76.

Odegaard, N. and O'Grady, C. R. 2016. The conservation practices for archaeological ceramics of Sir Flinders Petrie and others between 1880–1930. In Roemich, H. and Fair, L. (eds.) *Recent Advances in Glass and Ceramics Conservation 2016.* Paris: ICOM, Committee for Conservation, 85–95.

Parcak, S., Gathings, D., Childs, C., Mumford, G. and Cline, E. 2016. Satellite evidence of archaeological site looting in Egypt: 2002–2013. *Antiquity* 90: 188–205.

Parry, R. 2013. The end of the beginning: Normativity in the postdigital museum. *Museum Worlds: Advances in Research* 1(1): 24–39.

Peers, L. 2014. Source communities. *Pitt Rivers Museum Blog*, 31 January. https://pittrivers-americas.blogspot.com/2014/01/source-communities-back-in-july-at.html [Accessed 21 December 2021]

Peers, L. and Brown, A. 2003. Introduction. In Peers, L. and Brown, A. (eds.) *Museums and Source Communities.* London: Routledge, 1–16.

Pellizzi, F. 2008. Airports and museums: New frontiers of the urban and suburban. *RES: Anthropology and Aesthetics* 53(1): 331–44.

Petrie, W. M. F. 1888. *Tanis II.* London: Egypt Exploration Fund.

Petrie, W. M. F. 1890. *Kahun, Gurob, and Hawara.* London: Kegan Paul.

Petrie, W. M. F. 1899. Sequences in prehistoric remains. *Journal of the Anthropological Institute of Great Britain Ireland* 29: 295–301.

Petrie, W. M. F. 1904. *Methods and Aims in Archaeology.* London: Macmillan.

Petrie, W. M. F. and Brunton, G. 1924. *Sedment.* London: BSAE.

Phillips, R. B. 2002. Where is 'Africa'? Re-viewing art and artifact in the age of globalization. *American Anthropologist* 104(3): 944–52.

Phillips, R. B. 2011. *Museum Pieces: Toward the Indigenization of Canadian Museums.* Montreal and Kingston: McGill-Queens University Press.

Picton, J. and Pridden, I. (eds.) 2008. *Unseen Images: Archive Photographs in the Petrie Museum.* London: Golden House.

Pitkin, M. 2019. Pop-up museum in Cairo. *The Egyptian Coffins Project*, 24 July. https://egyptiancoffins.org/news/popupmuseum [Accessed 28 October 2021]

Pitt-Rivers, A. H. L. F. 1882. Scientific exploration in Egypt. *The Times*, 10 August, 10.

Pitt-Rivers, A. H. L. F. 1883. *On the Development and Distribution of Primitive Locks and Keys: Illustrated by Specimens in the Pitt Rivers Collection.* London: Chatto and Windus.

Price, C. 2020. *Golden Mummies of Egypt: Interpreting Identities from the Graeco-Roman Period.* Manchester: Manchester Museum.

Putnam, J. and Davies, V. (eds.) 1994. *Time Machine: Ancient Egypt and Contemporary Art.* Leeds: Jackson Wilson.

Pye, E. (ed.) 2007. *The Power of Touch: Handling Objects in Museum and Heritage Contexts*. London: Routledge.

Quinn, P. 2022. Scientific investigation of museum objects: Planning, analysis, and wider impact. In Stevenson, A. (ed.) *The Oxford Handbook of Museum Archaeology*. Oxford: Oxford University Press, 387–401.

Quirke, S. 2009. Petrie archives in London and Oxford. In Magee, D., Bourriau, J. and Quirke, S. (eds.) *Sitting Beside Lepsius: Studies in Honour of Jaromir Malek at the Griffith Institute*. Leuven: Peeters, 439–61.

Quirke, S. 2010. *Hidden Hands: Egyptian Workforces in Petrie Excavation Archives, 1880–1924*. London: Duckworth.

Rashed, M. G. 2015. The museums of Egypt after the 2011 revolution. *Museum International* 67: 125–31.

Rashed, M. G. and Bdr-El-Din, M. 2018. Documentation, object recording, and the role of curators in the Egyptian Museum, Cairo. *CiPEG Journal* 2: 41–63.

Regulski, I. 2018. The Rosetta Stone: Copying an ancient copy. In Davies, V. and Laboury, D. (eds.) *The Oxford Handbook of Egyptian Epigraphy and Paleography*. Oxford: Oxford University Press, 215-228.

Reid, D. 2002. *Whose Pharaohs? Archaeology, Museums, and Egyptian National Identity from Napoleon to World War I*. Berkeley: University of California Press.

Rhys, O. and Baveystock, Z. 2014. (eds.) *Collecting the Contemporary: A Handbook for Social History Museums*. Edinburgh: MuseumsEtc.

Richards, J. 2002. Text and context in late Old Kingdom Egypt: The archaeology and historiography of Weni the Elder. *Journal of the American Research Center in Egypt* 39: 79–102.

Riefstahl, E. 1953. Exhibitions of Egyptian material in the Brooklyn Museum. *Museum* 4(1): 31–35.

Riggs, C. 2010. Ancient Egypt in the museum: Concepts and constructions. In Lloyd, A. (ed.) *A Companion to Ancient Egypt*. Chichester: Blackwell, 1129–53.

Riggs, C. 2013. Colonial visions: Egyptian antiquities and contested histories in the Cairo Museum. *Museum Worlds: Advances in Research* 1: 65–84.

Riggs, C. 2014. *Unwrapping Ancient Egypt: The Shroud, the Secret and the Sacred*. London: Bloomsbury.

Riggs, C. 2016. The body in the box: Archiving the Egyptian mummy. *Archival Science: International Journal on Recorded Information* 17(2): 125–50.

Riggs, C. 2017a. *Egypt: Lost Civilizations*. London: Reaktion Books.

Riggs, C. 2017b. Shouldering the past: Photography, archaeology, and collective effort at the tomb of Tutankhamun. *History of Science* 55(3): 336–63.

Riggs, C. 2019. *Photographing Tutankhamun: Archaeology, Ancient Egypt, and the Archive*. London: Bloomsbury.

Riggs, C. 2020. Archaeology and photography. In Pasternak, G. (ed.) *The Handbook of Photography Studies*. London: Bloomsbury, 187–205.

Riggs, C. 2021. *Treasured: How Tutankhamun Shaped a Century*. London: Atlantic Books.

Roberts, L. A. 2013. The role of sculpture in communicating archaeology in museums. *Papers from the Institute of Archaeology* 23(1): article 6, 1–21.

Robillard, M. and Bahuchet, S. 2012. Les Pygmées et les autres: terminologie, catégorisation et politique. *Journal de la Société des Africanistes* 82(1–2): 15–51.

Robins, G. 2008. *Ancient Egyptian Art*. Cambridge, MA: Harvard University Press.

Robinson, E. 1903. Report of the director. *Annual Report for the Year (Museum of Fine Arts, Boston)* 28: 40–7.

Rothberg, M. 2009. *Multidirectional Memory: Remembering the Holocaust in the Age of Decolonization*. Paolo Alto: Stanford University Press.

Rothberg, M. 2014. Multidirectional memory. *Témoigner: Entre histoire et mémoire* 119: 172–83. https://doi.org/10.4000/temoigner.1494.

Russman, E. R. 2001. *Eternal Egypt: Masterworks of Ancient Art from the British Museum*. London: British Museum Press.

Said, E. 1978. *Orientalism*. New York: Pantheon Books.

Saini, A. 2019. *Superior: The Return of Race Science*. Boston: Beacon Press.

Savage, S. 2001. Some recent trends in the archaeology of Predynastic Egypt. *Journal of Archaeological Research* 9(2): 101–55.

Schneider, T. 2007. Foreign Egypt: Egyptology and the concept of cultural appropriation. *Ägypten & Levante* 13: 155–61.

Schneider, T. 2008. Periodizing Egyptian history: Manetho, convention, and beyond. In Adam, K.-P. (ed.) *Historiographie in der Antike*. Berlin: De Gruyter, 183–97.

Schoske, S. and Wildung, D. 1983. *Falsche Faraonen: Zeitung zur Sonderaustellung 400 Jahrae Fälschungsgeschichte*. Munich: Die Sammlung.

Serotta, A. 2014. An investigation of tool marks on ancient Egyptian hard stone sculpture: Preliminary report. *Metropolitan Museum Studies in Art Science and Technology* 2: 197–201.

Shalem, A. 2012. Multivalent paradigms of interpretation and aura or anima of the object. In Junod, B., Khalil, G., Weber, S. and Wolf, G. (eds.) *Islamic Art and the Museum*. London: Saqi Books, 101–15.

Shatanawi, M. 2021. Museum narratives of Islam between art, archaeology and ethnology: A structural injustice approach. In Puzon, K., Macdonald, S. and

Shatanawi, M. (eds.) *Islam and Heritage in Europe*. London: Routledge, 163–82.

Shaya, J. 2021. Lingering tropes and noteworthy narratives in recent archaeology exhibitions. *American Journal of Archaeology* 125(4): 639–55.

Shelton, A. 2000. Curating African worlds. *Journal of Museum Ethnography* 12: 5–20.

Sheppard, K. 2010. Flinders Petrie and eugenics. *Bulletin of the History of Archaeology* 20(1): 16–29.

Silverman, M. 2013. *Palimpsestic Memory: The Holocaust and Colonialism in French and Francophone Fiction and Film*. New York: Berghahn Books.

Skeates, R. and Day, J. (eds.) 2019. *The Routledge Handbook of Sensory Archaeology*. London: Routledge.

Stable, C., Maitland, M., de Bellalgue, D. et al. 2021. Rediscovering ancient Egypt: Consideration of the legacy, ethics and aesthetics of previously restored Egyptian artefacts. *Journal of the Institute of Conservation* 44(2): 134–52.

Stevenson, A. 2009. *The Predynastic Egyptian Cemetery of El-Gerzeh*. Leuven: Peeters.

Stevenson, A. 2015a. Early experiments: A view from the Pitt Rivers Museum. In Graves-Brown, C. (ed.) *Egyptology in the Present: Experiential and Experimental Methods in Archaeology*. Swansea: Classical Press of Wales, 151–71.

Stevenson, A. 2015b. Telling times: Time and ritual in the formation of the Egyptian state. *Cambridge Archaeological Journal* 25(1): 145–61.

Stevenson, A. 2019. *Scattered Finds: Archaeology, Egyptology and Museums*. London: UCL Press.

Stevenson, A., Libonati, E. and Baines, J. 2017. The object habit. *Museum History Journal* 10(2): 113–26.

Stevenson, A. and Williams, A. In press. Blind-spots in museum anthropology: Ancient Egypt in the ethnographic museum. *Museum Anthropology*.

Sweetnam, E. and Henderson, J. 2022. Disruptive conservation: Challenging conservation orthodoxy. *Studies in Conservation* 67(1–2): 63–71.

Swift, E., Stoner, J. and Pudsey, A. 2021. *A Social Archaeology of Roman and Late Antique Egypt: Artefacts of Everyday Life*. Oxford: Oxford University Press.

Szántó, A. 2020. *The Future of the Museum: 28 Dialogues*. Berlin: Hantje Cantz.

Thomas, N. 2016. *The Return of Curiosity: What Museums are Good for in the Twenty-First Century*. London: Reaktion Books.

Thum, J. and Troche, J. 2016. Visitor as researcher: Making archaeology more accessible with broken and unprovenienced objects. *Advances in Archaeological Practice* 4(4): 537–49.

Tian, T. 2021. Thoth with four eyes: Chinese views of Egyptian hieroglyphs in late Qing period (1840–1912). *Journal of Ancient Egyptian Interconnections* 31: 55–80.

Trafton, S. 2004. *Egypt Land: Race and Nineteenth-Century American Egyptomania.* Durham: Duke University Press.

Tuck, E. and Yang, K. W. 2012. Decolonization is not a metaphor. *Decolonization: Indigeneity, Education and Society* 1(1): 1–40.

Tully, G. 2017. Re-imagining Egypt: Artefacts, contemporary art and community engagement in the museum. In Onciul, B., Stefano, M. L. and Hawke, S. (eds.) *Engaging Heritage, Engaging Communities.* Woodbridge: The Boydell Press, 91–106.

Turner, H. 2020. *Cataloguing Culture: Legacies of Colonialism in Museum Documentation.* Vancouver: UBC Press.

Van Broekhoven, L. N. K. 2018. Calibrating relevance at the Pitt Rivers Museum. In Pellew, J. and Goldman, L. (eds.) *Dethroning Historical Reputations: Universities, Museums and the Commemoration of Benefactors.* London: School of Advanced Study, 65–79.

Vergo, P. 1989. *The New Museology.* London: Reaktion.

Versluys, M. J. (ed.) 2020. *Beyond Egyptomania: Objects, Style and Agency.* Berlin: De Gruyter.

Wedge, E. F. (ed.) 1977. *Nefertiti Graffiti: Comments on an Exhibition.* Brooklyn: The Brooklyn Museum.

Weiss, L. 2018. Aesthetics and science: The new permanent Egyptian galleries in the Leiden National Museum of Antiquities. *Aegyptiaca: Journal of the History of the Reception of Ancient Egypt* 2: 213–34.

Wessel, G. 2015. Dealers, collectors, provenances and rights: Searching for traces. In Desmarais, F. (ed.) *Countering Illicit Traffic in Cultural Goods: The Global Challenge of Protecting the World's Heritage.* Paris: ICOM, 1–10.

Whitehouse, H. 1989. The case of the Bodleian shabti. *Journal of the History of Collections* 1(2): 187–95.

Whitley, J. 2016. Discussion and debate: Fusing the horizons, or why context matters: The interdependence of fieldwork and museum study in Mediterranean archaeology. *Journal of Mediterranean Archaeology* 29(2): 247–61.

Wilfong, T. G. 2010. Gender in ancient Egypt. In Wendrich, W. (ed.) *Egyptian Archaeology.* Chichester: Blackwell, 164–79.

Wilfong, T. G. 2012. The University of Michigan excavation of Karanis (1924–1935): Images from the Kelsey Museum photographic archives. In Riggs, C. (ed.) *The Oxford Handbook of Roman Egypt.* Oxford: Oxford University Press, 226–41.

Wilfong, T. G. 2014. The sonic landscape of Karanis: Excavating the sounds of a village in Roman Egypt. In Wilfong, T. G. and Ferrara, A. W. (eds.) *Karanis Revealed: Discovering the Past and Present of a Michigan Excavation in Egypt*. Ann Arbor: Kelsey Museum of Archaeology, 169–78.

Wray, D. 2021. Egyptology's eloquent eye: Mohammedani Ibrahim. *Aramco World*, September/October. www.aramcoworld.com/Articles/September-2021/ Egyptology-s-Eloquent-Eye [Accessed 21 December 2021]

Zinn, K. 2018. Did you sleep well on your headrest? Anthropological perspectives on an ancient Egyptian implement. *Journal of Ancient Egyptian Interconnections* 17: 202–19.

Zinn, K. 2019. The museum of lies: Incorrect facts or advancing knowledge of ancient Egypt. *Journal of History and Cultures* 10: 165–90.

Acknowledgements

I am grateful to colleagues for answering queries, as well as advising on readings, collections, and images including Paige Brevick, Stuart Frost, Rachel Mairs, Laura Osorio Sunnucks, Luigi Prada, Pamela Rose, Amanda Ford Spora, Paolo del Vesco, and Alice Williams. Special thanks go to Anna Garnett and Margaret Maitland for comments on earlier drafts of this text, as well as to Heba Abd el-Gawad for advice and for introducing me to the work of Gamal Hamdan. Thanks also to Gianluca Miniaci and an anonymous reviewer for helpful further guidance.

Cambridge Elements ≡

Ancient Egypt in Context

Gianluca Miniaci
University of Pisa

Gianluca Miniaci is Associate Professor in Egyptology at the University of Pisa, Honorary Researcher at the Institute of Archaeology, UCL – London, and Chercheur associé at the École Pratique des Hautes Études, Paris. He is currently co-director of the archaeological mission at Zawyet Sultan (Menya, Egypt). His main research interest focusses on the social history and the dynamics of material culture in the Middle Bronze Age Egypt and its interconnections between the Levant, Aegean, and Nubia.

Juan Carlos Moreno García
CNRS, Paris

Juan Carlos Moreno García (PhD in Egyptology, 1995) is a CNRS senior researcher at the University of Paris IV-Sorbonne, as well as lecturer on social and economic history of ancient Egypt at the École des Hautes Études en Sciences Sociales (EHESS) in Paris. He has published extensively on the administration, socio-economic history, and landscape organization of ancient Egypt, usually in a comparative perspective with other civilizations of the ancient world, and has organized several conferences on these topics.

Anna Stevens
University of Cambridge and Monash University

Anna Stevens is a research archaeologist with a particular interest in how material culture and urban space can shed light on the lives of the non-elite in ancient Egypt. She is Senior Research Associate at the McDonald Institute for Archaeological Research and Assistant Director of the Amarna Project (both University of Cambridge).

About the Series

The aim of this Elements series is to offer authoritative but accessible overviews of foundational and emerging topics in the study of ancient Egypt, along with comparative analyses, translated into a language comprehensible to non-specialists. Its authors will take a step back and connect ancient Egypt to the world around, bringing ancient Egypt to the attention of the broader humanities community and leading Egyptology in new directions.

Cambridge Elements⁼

Ancient Egypt in Context

Elements in the Series

Printed in the United States
by Baker & Taylor Publisher Services